We all have a purpose for being here

a memoir

by
Jean Hendrickson

Best wishes,
Jean Hendrickson

Illumina
PUBLISHING
Friday Harbor, Washington

© 2005 Jean Hendrickson. All rights reserved
Revised in 2007

No part of this book may be used or reproduced in any manner whatsoever without written permission except in the case of brief quotations embodied in critical reviews and certain other non-commercial uses permitted by copyright law.

Illumina Publishing, Friday Harbor, Washington 98250
Printed by LightningSource
in the United States of America

Library of Congress Cataloging-in-Publication Data
Hendrickson, Jean
We all Have a Purpose For Being Here - A Memoir

ISBN: 0-9718600-4-1
    978-0-9718600-4-9

Layout, cover and book design by Bruce Conway, Friday Harbor, WA
Cover painting by Willow Rose, Friday Harbor, WA
Cover photography by Jane Buck
Copy editing: Jane Alynn, Anacortes, WA
Orca photos courtesy of www.carliwhalewatch.com

For Sharon
— with much love
and gratitude for all
your pioneering work
and your friendship.
   Love, Jean

(see p. 55)

Dedication

To my beloved friend, Pat Pedersen

Acknowledgments

There are so many people for whom I feel great appreciation and indebtedness for their love, support, and encouragement throughout my lifetime. Many of them will remain nameless, for fear I may inadvertently leave out any of these dear friends and mentors. I thank them all with great love. Because of them I have had a rich and very rewarding life.

At this point in time, I am particularly grateful to all those who have encouraged me to write this book and who have been willing to read the first drafts and offer suggestions. Their advice has been invaluable, and I thank them from the bottom of my heart. Especially I include in this list Deborah Neff, Pat Pedersen, Ann Schwarz, Tom Heye, Jim Haney, Mark Gibson, Janet Thomas, Forrest Rollins, Deborah Thompson, Thrinley DiMarco, and Krysta Gibson.

Special thanks go to my production team. It was a delight to work with Bruce Conway, who designed and prepared my book for publication. Since this was a new experience for me, his creativity and expertise were essential to the completion of this project. Bruce and I have been friends for many years, and he has consistently supported the publication of my story. For this I am most grateful.

Special thanks also go to proofreader Jen Conway, copy editor Jane Alynn, and Willow Rose, who painted the marvelous landscape featured on the cover of this book.

I also want to acknowledge and thank my parents—Warren and Connie Soule, my sister Marian, Grandma Jo, Austin, Viena, Raenay, and my grandchildren—Deon, Haeley, Erick, and Alana. I thank all of the teachers and people who believed in me, challenged me, and inspired me. I thank all my loving friends who have continued to support me, encourage me, and share the adventures with me. And I thank all my clients over the years, from whom I learned so much, even as the spiritual energy and guidance that flowed through me for their growth and healing assisted each of them.

I especially want to acknowledge and thank my three children—Susan, Grant, and Sharon. Each had their own special dreams and opportunities. They had the courage to explore these opportunities and to express themselves. When I was in my early forties, I knew that I had some kind of mission to fulfill. They didn't protest when I needed to follow my own visions and knowings about what I wanted and needed to do. Often they didn't understand what I was doing and why I was doing it, but they didn't try to interfere or persuade me in another direction. For this, I am deeply grateful.

Above all, I want to thank, from deep in my heart, all those loving and beautiful souls in the other dimensions who have guided and directed me throughout my life. I didn't recognize and identify them until I was in my mid-forties, but I know they have been with me and walked every step of the way with me. They have orchestrated innumerable events in order to facilitate my growth and prepare me to carry out my purpose in this lifetime. I have been but an instrument of the Divine, and they have provided the guidance that has allowed me to fulfill my purpose.

Thanks to all of you!

Contents

Acknowledgments 5

Introduction 9

Chapter 1   The Beginnings 15

Chapter 2   Marriage, Motherhood and Community 25

Chapter 3   Women's Clinic, University, Women's Shelter 49

Chapter 4   Eight Years of Intense Spiritual Growth 67

Chapter 5   Seattle and Sedona 103

Chapter 6   San Juan Island 135

Chapter 7   Looking Back, Looking Forward 161

Epilogue 197

Jean's Article: "How To Deal With The Changes" 207

Jean's Morning Alignment, Prayers and Meditation 212

Recommended Resources 214

Healing Resources 217

Introduction

My memoir began to unfold in the spring of 2003. My original intent was to share my spiritual experiences with others who are beginning this journey or who need encouragement to continue on their spiritual journey. It would be my way of offering support to those who would choose a path of spiritual growth and service. There have been many people over the years who have told me that I should write down my stories, but, quite frankly, I didn't have a clue where to start a project of this magnitude or how to proceed. I secretly hoped that someone would take an interest in this project, and with recorder in hand I would share my life story. That person would then assemble the book. Well, it never happened the way I imagined.

As divine orchestration would have it, an extension course was offered at our community college entitled "Writing Your Memoir." It was taught by a friend and published writer, Janet Thomas, who was looking for an eighth student. I enrolled as the eighth student, and two more followed. I learned that there are no rules in writing a memoir. I liked that! Our class had writing assignments on a weekly basis, which we read out loud to the class. These assignments stretched and opened me to many aspects of my life I had forgotten about or deemed unimportant. This was just the gentle nudge I needed to start writing my memoir.

This spiritual journey, which began in my early forties, continues to unfold beautifully as divinely orchestrated. It has been an extraordinary journey, and one for which I am enormously grateful. My spiritual growth and commitment continue to be the priority in my life, and I share my stories with the deepest love and compassion for all others. It is my desire that these stories will serve to assist, encourage, uplift, and console.

During my life I have learned that there are only two reasons that we come into these bodies on the earth plane—to learn and to serve—and we learn by serving. We all have a purpose for being here, and as we progress throughout our lives we are guided by our Higher Selves and our spiritual guides to create opportunities for our learning and to unfold aspects of our purpose for being here. In looking back at my life, I have come to know that everything I have experienced has had a purpose. My childhood, my marriage and motherhood, and all of the activities in my life prior to my spiritual awakening have been important in my learning. Thus, I have written about these earlier events because the spiritual experiences I share could be more meaningful given a context in which to relate them.

Also, as I began to write, I became aware of many aspects of my life for which I now have a much greater appreciation and acceptance. I have told many people that I have had a wonderful life—not an easy one but a very interesting one. There have been circumstances which felt like disasters and made me anxious, only to have a totally unexpected resolution that later proved to be the perfect outcome. Now I value in a deeper way the times of hardship and challenge, for they have helped to sculpt and create who I have become. So I have learned to give thanks in advance for the perfect solution of difficult situations, knowing that it truly will happen, even if I don't comprehend it in the moment.

These days I feel an expanded level of gratitude for all of these experiences, and for each person who has inspired me, provided the lessons that have stretched my awareness, and encouraged, supported, and cared for me along the way. I am also grateful for all those who have shared the adventures with me, the fun and laughter that have nurtured me. There are countless people who have blessed me beyond measure; many of them are not aware that they have done so. I have intentionally not named most of them in my story and in some cases I have changed their names, in part, to preserve their privacy, but also because I did not want to inadvertently omit the names of precious friends and teachers who have given me great support, joy, love, and encouragement.

As I have been looking back on my life, I have had a much fuller realization that my life has unfolded in a way that I could never have planned in advance. Marvelous opportunities have presented themselves, and a spiritual guidance I could not have predicted has been operating all along. I have also been privileged to live in a period of time in our country that has experienced phenomenal change. I was born in 1928, lived through the Great Depression, the Second World War and all of its atrocities, the introduction and expansion of incredible new technologies, and the development of suburban sprawl. I was very active in the peace movement; I protested the war in Vietnam and worked for disarmament. I also witnessed and participated in the civil rights and women's rights movements, helping to pioneer many new services. It was in the latter half of the last century that spiritual development and spiritual healing began to flourish in a new way. A large number of new systems were taught and practiced. I spent many years working as a counselor and teaching spiritual healing. What an extraordinary period in history!

For several years I have had a beautiful and meaningful quotation on my refrigerator door: "We are not human beings having a spiritual experience. We are spiritual beings having a human experience," written by Teilhard de Chardin. I have clearly learned that this is true. I know we are not separate from other people or from any other form of life on earth. Twenty years ago I had a profound experience of "oneness" with all that is in creation. This experience forever changed me. I also have learned that our earth is going through massive frequency changes on an energy level in preparation for a transformation of consciousness on our planet. As Mother Earth moves ever closer to the completion of a major cycle of evolution and prepares for her birthing into her new cycle of consciousness, it is mandatory that the vibrational frequency on the planet be raised to levels far beyond anything that has been experienced here before. This is being accomplished by infusions of energy directed to the Earth, and these infusions come in small increments, like drops, at regular intervals. Some of them feel more intense than others, but every aspect of us is being affected by these new higher frequencies.

We have now moved into the intense and crucial phase of our planet's evolution, so we are being challenged to our core. We experience these challenges not only physically but also emotionally and mentally. My primary spiritual work during the last two decades has been to serve as a "transformer" for these higher frequencies for the earth, and my body has gone through massive changes in order to assist the grounding of these energies. Vast multitudes of us have chosen to become human beings to assist the earth and humanity in this process of transformation. The energy frequencies have been raised, in stages, as we are ready for them, and we have assisted in grounding these vibrations. In order to do this, our physical bodies have had to undergo changes at a cellular level so that our vibratory rates can be increased. This restructuring or transforming of our physical bodies is preparation for each of us to handle the higher vibrations.

All of us are in preparation for assuming our roles of leadership in the coming months and years. No one's role, or purpose, is more important than any other because we each have a unique way to be of service. Some will be quite public, whereas others will be very quiet and unobtrusive instruments by their example of kindness, peacefulness, gentleness, faith, and joy. Some will do this in a personal and individual way, and others will come together in groups or communities to accomplish the work at hand. All of it is important. Ultimately, I believe the transformation must include the emergence of a world where there are no more wars and where people have learned to live in harmony and peace. The way to peace is to choose love, forgiveness, and compassion over fear, revenge, and a quest for power.

Love is the transforming agent, and it begins with ourselves. Releasing our judgments is the key to loving ourselves and others. When we judge anyone, including ourselves, we restrict the flow of love to ourselves and others. We all came into these bodies, these human experiences, with two givens: we are equally loved by the Creator, and we are equally worthy. Each of us makes mistakes, as that is part of the human experience. It is painful to observe the violence, greed, and the destruction of our environment that is taking place on our beautiful planet. But if we judge ourselves for our mistakes or condemn the perpetrators of destructive behavior, we will have closed our hearts and love will be restricted. I grew up with considerable abuse in my childhood, and I have had to work through layers of fear, anger, judgment, and painful memories to find true peace, joy, and love. It is possible, and each step that we take in our own personal growth ultimately benefits all of humankind. The transformation on earth will ultimately be accomplished with love.

It is likely that most people's spiritual lives have roots even before they know the roots are there. Although I didn't know it then, my roots started in my childhood and continued on into my early adulthood. If your interest in reading my story is primarily related to spiritual growth, how it unfolded for me and what I have learned, then you might just skip over the first three chapters of my early history. My desire is that my story will help others to feel encouraged and inspired to keep on with their journey, in spite of the obstacles in their path. If that happens, then this book will have served a purpose. I truly know that all of our experiences are important, there are no accidents, and each of us has come in with a purpose and a reason for being here.

Chapter 1
The Beginnings

As I begin the writing of my memoir, it is the springtime of 2003, and I have just celebrated my seventy-fifth birthday. I suspect most young adults would consider seventy-five to be quite old. Definitely retirement age. But I started a whole new and very successful career as a wedding officiant when I was sixty-seven, which is still enormously enjoyable for me, and it is flourishing. For the first time in my life I played a principal role in a play and sang a solo on stage when I was seventy. I have played a creative part in pioneering several new services in our country. I have always expected new adventures would unfold throughout my life, and they have. It has been exciting and rewarding for me. Now I'm about to embark on what might be the greatest adventure of my entire life. I truly am excited!

My home is on a stunningly beautiful island in northwestern Washington State. My spiritual guides orchestrated my move to this island over twelve years ago. From various vantage points on the island I can see Mount Baker and the Cascade Mountains to the east, the Olympic Mountains to the south, and the southern tip of Vancouver Island and Victoria to the west. There is a feeling of magic when you live on an island surrounded by ocean water.

I love this island. Here, orca whales, eagles and other wild life, its awesome natural beauty, the climate, and all of my wonderful friends and activities sustain me. I never anticipated that I would leave. However, I have recently been guided and connected with many others with whom I will participate in creating a new spiritual center in Costa Rica for the transformation of consciousness on our planet. This project will be located on sacred land in an exquisite area in the mountains of Costa Rica. But first, let me share some background.

One of the sweet advantages of living to be seventy-five is that you can look back on your life and see patterns emerging. You can't see them when you are younger and living them. It requires some distance. I have lived through many traumas and wounding. At the same time I have also been blessed with an abundance of beautiful friends, a lovely family, happy accomplishments, recognition, creative fulfillment and fun. But the hard stuff is what creates the strength, understanding, and ability to take risks. At this point in my life I am truly grateful for all of the challenges and the pain I have endured, and for the incredible opportunities they gave me.

I was born and raised in Minneapolis, Minnesota. Having been born on the spring equinox in 1928, I grew up during the Great Depression in this country. It was a struggle for my parents, financially and in other ways. We were definitely poor, and there was money only for the most basic necessities of life. Even as a young child, I was aware of my mother's fear about not having enough money. This one memory is still vivid. It was winter, which in Minnesota is often very cold. My father was away selling a variety of products for a company and sending money home for the family as he was able. I was about five years old and my sister, Marian, was about three, when my mother asked us if she should spend our last fifty cents on milk, bread, or coal for the stove. In this lifetime I have never had very much money, but I can hardly imagine being so desperate that you would ask your young children to help you make such a decision. Still, I'm deeply aware this remains the reality for many people in our country and all over the world.

My father and mother came from vastly different backgrounds, and their personalities were as unlike as you can imagine. My mother grew up on a farm in Wisconsin. Her mother died when she was seven, and her father died when she was eleven. Then orphaned, she and her three siblings lived with older half brothers and half sisters until mother was fourteen, at which time she started living and working for her room and board with another family. She went to school, but after school she cared for the other family's children, cooking and cleaning for the family.

Mother was always a hard worker. She graduated from high school and went on to complete a year of what was called Normal School. That qualified her to teach in a small one-room rural grade school, which she did from age nineteen until she married my father at age twenty-three. From all that I have learned, life was indeed a struggle for her. I doubt that she had a role model for a mother. Mother seemed to be shy and uncomfortable in social situations, and she never wanted to call attention to herself. She was conservative, traditional, and always concerned about what other people would think. Every day I heard her say, "What will people say," if we did or said something of which she disapproved. She was totally rigid about how everything was to be done in our home. There was only one right way to wash dishes, scrub the floors, and do all other household chores. Her home was her haven, and there were rules about everything. Church was an essential element in her life, and therefore, we all had no choice but to attend. She was adamant about telling the truth. I think she worried about everything.

On the other hand, my father was born into a wealthy family. He, too, had three siblings, and apparently quite indulgent parents. They lived in a beautiful big house, took expensive vacations, and had many luxuries. He told me he got bored in high school and decided to quit when he was in eleventh grade. His parents did not protest and, to my knowledge, he did not finish high school. He was flamboyant, and I think he enjoyed being a playboy. My mother and father were married in 1927.

When the stock market crashed in 1929, my dad's father lost almost all of his wealth. I never heard conversations about what happened, but it was obvious when they moved out of the big house. My family lived in a very small one-bedroom home, and my paternal grandparents, Grandma Jo and Grandpa, lived in a small two-story bungalow. Grandma Jo's two sisters and Grandpa's brother all lived with them as well; thus I had some extended family but no cousins in the immediate area. During the Depression, it was common for families to group together to quite literally survive.

My dad was an incurable optimist and always believed everything was going to be better tomorrow. Telling the truth was not a virtue of my father. He bragged frequently and was always trying to impress other people, often by saying things that weren't true. It embarrassed me many times. In spite of losing all the wealth and privileges of his youth, his outlook on life was upbeat. When I became an adult and could understand more easily what life was like for him, I really appreciated and honored him for staying with his family and providing for their support in the best way that he could. He, too, turned out to be a hard worker.

My sister, Marian, and I had different personalities as well. I was more outgoing, and she was very introverted. For those interested in astrology, my sun and moon are in Pisces, and my rising sign is Leo. Therefore, I could be an effective leader and performer, and at other times be very shy. That still continues. I tended to have many more friends than Marian and liked to try new things. Marian was bright and a good student, but was more apt to stay alone, and never wanted to perform or take leadership.

My faith and optimism about the future I clearly received from my father; my honoring of being truthful, dependable, and religious were traits I received from my mother.

My mother criticized almost everything I did as a child, and she abused me physically, psychologically, and emotionally. The physical abuse was mostly slapping and spanking; she never injured me seriously. However, I rarely felt safe around her and was continually trying to please her. I do not remember succeeding very often, and the abuse would frequently come when I least expected it. As a result my self confidence suffered when I was a young child. My father was rarely abusive, except when I reached puberty, but I think he found it so difficult to be around my mother's nearly constant nagging that he chose to be away from home a lot. He was not there to protect Marian and me. I have no memories of either of my parents holding me on their laps to cuddle or to read to me.

Grandma Jo was the primary nurturing family member in my life. Since my mother's parents had died when she was very young, Grandma Jo and my grandfather were the only grandparents I knew. Although a tiny person, she would hold me on her lap and tell me I was a good girl and she loved me. When I came to her house, she would let me play "dress up" and wear her clothes, shoes, and jewelry. I loved going to be with her, and I felt safe there.

Jean's mother and father *Jean, Marian and Grandma Jo*

Grandma and Grandpa had an old but very good upright piano at their house, and I would play around on the keys whenever I could. When I was about seven or eight years old, they had the piano moved to my parents' home. Somehow my parents managed to pay for piano lessons for me, for which I am so grateful. My neighborhood piano teacher and I became good friends, and she continued to teach me even when my parents had no money to pay her. As I got a little older, sometimes I could pay her a little with money I earned from baby-sitting. When I turned sixteen and got a good part-time job in a big department store downtown, I paid for my piano lessons and for pipe organ lessons as well. I studied classical music for ten years and also sang in the church choir.

My grandfather became ill and died when I was sixteen. Grandma Jo then moved to our home and lived with us until she later decided to move to California. (A few years prior to that time my parents were able to buy an older three-bedroom home.) At that time I was taking piano lessons. We lived next door to the parsonage of a large church one block from our home, and the minister often heard me practicing the piano. Sometimes we talked out in the yard, and one day he asked me if I would like to play the organ. When I eagerly said "yes," he offered me the opportunity to learn to play their church's organ if I would take lessons there from the church organist. He gave me a key to the side door of the church so that I could go in and practice whenever there were no church activities taking place. I was thrilled to have that opportunity.

Often I would go to the church in the evening, turn on a light in the choir loft, and sit alone in that large, beautiful gothic sanctuary and practice the organ. It was an outstanding pipe organ, and I could play as loud as I wanted to. How I loved it. I have many precious memories of my sweet little grandmother quietly slipping in through the door she knew would be unlocked and listening to me play. I usually didn't hear her come in, but when I caught a glimpse of her sitting in one of the pews I would start playing her favorite song—Schubert's Serenade.

Playing the piano was really the only thing I did for which my mother showed approval. I practiced more than an hour a day because I wanted to, and she would sometimes say something complimentary to me about my diligence. What she didn't know was that playing the piano was how I dealt with my emotions in relation to her. It was never safe to show anger to my mother; that would result in more abuse. So I played the piano. Big, loud and dramatic concertos especially enabled me to release my anger. Not only was the piano my haven, playing brought approval and recognition at church and a few other places. I was asked to play fairly often, and I was especially good at accompanying other musicians and playing for group singing. I really liked this, and it boosted my self-esteem.

Most of my close friends were members of our church. I was very active in the high school group and was president for one year. The parents of my church friends were warm and welcoming to me, and I felt accepted. I especially looked forward to the week-long summer camp programs, which were nurturing experiences. When I went to the summer camps I decided to drop my first name. My parents named me Vella Jean Soule. I disliked the name Vella, and people often mispronounced it. So I told my new camp friends that my name was Jean. My parents were upset when my new friends called me on the phone and asked for Jean, but it stuck, and I have carried the name of Jean ever since.

In my teen years I made a choice to prepare for a career in church service of some kind. I took seriously the teachings of Jesus about love, and I got very upset when I heard my parents, especially my father, make disparaging remarks about people of other races and religious faiths. He frequently referred to Jews as "kikes" and black people as "niggers." This bothered me a lot, and I remember having some major arguments with my father about this at the dinner table when I was a junior and senior in high school. My mother usually didn't say much, but she didn't try to prevent the conversation. I think I was starting to move into my power.

About that time I went with some high school friends from my local church to a week-long summer ecumenical church camp in Wisconsin. We were assigned roommates by the camp staff, and when I moved into my room I discovered my roommate was a very dark-skinned black girl from Indiana. She was friendly, and I liked her immediately. It was my first personal connection with a black person, since there were no black people at my school or church, and I was a little uncomfortable at first when a couple of her black friends came to our room to see my roommate. For the first time I was the only white person present. During the week I got to know those three black girls quite well, as they often included me in activities during our free-time periods. It was fun to hear their stories, and it didn't seem to be any big deal for them to include me in the group. Looking back, this was the early foundation that prepared me to later work for civil rights in this country.

As a child, I was always drawn to nature. No one else in my family seemed to be particularly interested. We lived in a house that was only three blocks from a lake in South Minneapolis. When I was old enough, my mother let me walk to the lake by myself. I would hang out with the big, old trees by the water. Some of them leaned out over the water, and I had a favorite one that I climbed on where I could sit for hours. Occasionally I took a fishing pole, and once in awhile I would catch a little sunfish or two. One time when I took some fish home, my mother cleaned them and cooked them for me. That was a special treat and a precious memory I have of my mother.

My mother's brother and his wife, Uncle John and Aunt Mabel, lived on the family farm in Wisconsin where my mother grew up. It was about seventy-five miles from Minneapolis. They had two children, my cousins Bob and Joan. My mother's sister, Aunt Florence, her husband, Uncle Eyner, and their family—my cousins Bonnie and Doug, lived near the farm also. My parents had an old car and we did not go places very often, so it was a big event when we went to visit the farm in Wisconsin where I could be with all my cousins. There was lots of laughter and caring interactions, all of which were in short supply in my family home. A couple of summers I spent a week on the farm without my parents.

It felt nourishing to me to be at the farm. My cousins, the animals, the huge fields of corn, hay, and other grains, the vegetable garden, all the aromas, and fresh air were a delight to me. Everyone worked hard on the farm, including the kids, but for me it didn't feel like work. It was more like play. Joan and I helped Aunt Mabel prepare food, wash dishes, and do all sorts of farm chores. Uncle John taught me how to milk a cow, and he let me ride on the work horses when he was cultivating the fields. They didn't have power machinery in those days. An especially exciting time for me was "haying." Farmers from neighboring farms came and helped Uncle John harvest his hay fields. They brought the hay bales to the barn to be stored in the hay loft for winter feed for the livestock. The farmers joked and laughed, and I really enjoyed their camaraderie. The whole process was fascinating to me, and my love of nature deepened.

When I was a teen-ager, I intended to prepare myself to go on to college. I didn't know how I would pay for it, but that was clearly my intention. At the end of ninth grade, as I was preparing my high school schedule of classes, I was devastated when my father insisted that I take the intensive secretarial training course in high school. I didn't want to be a secretary. But my father's adamant position was that no child of his was going to graduate from high school without being prepared to immediately get a job. He insisted on accompanying me to a conference with the school counselor in charge of the high school schedule. He got his way, and I had to drop several academic courses I had intended to take. It infuriated me even more when Marian, who was almost two years younger than I, was preparing her high school schedule, and he did not make that demand of her. Looking back over my life now, I am grateful for his interference, for those secretarial skills have served me very well in many situations. And they still do. I now think it was one of those divine manipulations.

After graduation from high school, I did not have the money or enough academic credits to go to college. I got a job immediately as a legal secretary in a small law office, and I took two night school academic courses that entire next year. I lived at home and saved my earnings. During that year I met Austin at our Christian church. He was the nephew of the choir director and his wife, and he had recently finished his three and one-half years of service in the Navy during World War II. Fortunately, he was not called for overseas duty during his military service. I had dated several boys during high school, but none of them were serious relationships. Even though Austin was nearly seven years older than I, we began to date, and over the next year our relationship grew. I learned a great deal from his experiences in college and the Navy.

The following year, at age nineteen, I entered Macalester College, a small but outstanding liberal arts college in St. Paul. My parents allowed me to live at home without paying for room and board, but they had no money to help me with college expenses. It was a long bus ride from home in Minneapolis to the campus in St. Paul—a minimum of one hour, with two transfers—so I usually studied during the ride. I carried a sack lunch with me to save the expense of buying lunch. Because I could not live on the campus, I missed out on many of the social events. I remember that I had four goals for that first year in college: to get four As, to learn to play bridge, to drink coffee, and to smoke. I got four As, learned to play bridge, and drank coffee, but I couldn't stand smoking. I tried it for about three weeks or so and could never allow myself to inhale because it felt like such violence to my lungs. So I decided to quit and have never smoked again. I'm grateful for that decision. In March of that year, on my 20th birthday, Austin gave me an engagement ring.

Following that first college year, I found a good paying secretarial job for the summer, which provided the needed funds to pay for one more college semester. I knew when I started college that I would probably not be able to attend for more than two years. I was thrilled with my college experiences, and they had great impact on my life. My college advisor put in special efforts to enroll me in classes taught by what she called "the great minds of the college." For example, she was able to persuade the head of the philosophy department to allow me to take his introductory philosophy course (which was for juniors and seniors) during the second semester of my freshman year. Those professors and classes provided me with a basis for learning how to think, how to search for what I wanted to learn, and to be discerning. They greatly broadened my awareness of other cultures and philosophies. As a result, my vision and sense of purpose grew enormously.

Looking back, I am also aware of the privilege I had in attending a college where the classes were small. It provided a great deal of discussion and interaction between students and teachers. I had worked hard to save the money for college, and I had grown up a lot during that year after high school, so I was very serious about getting all I could from college. In 1947, when I started at Macalester, most American colleges and universities were flooded with veterans who were now home from the war and who were able to attend college on the GI Bill. These veterans were older than freshman right out of high school, and they also were serious about their education. Their experiences in the war had created a level of maturity that most of the eighteen-year-olds did not have, so there were many in-depth discussions in classes. I can see now how orchestrated it was for me to spend the extra money to attend Macalester rather than to be in large classes at the University of Minnesota. It was another chapter in my life for which I am grateful.

Chapter 2

Marriage—Motherhood—Community

During the summer after my first year in college, Austin and I decided to be married. After the war there was a huge shortage of housing, and many couples did not get married until they found a place to live. A friend of mine at Macalester College learned about a widow who lived a mile from the college and who was renting part of her home. After seeing it, we decided to take it and to get married. We planned our church wedding in three weeks so that we could be married in late August before I went back to college, and so that our wedding would not interfere with a trip my parents had scheduled. This was a major decision, and a bit scary for me, but it felt right. It was a beautiful evening wedding.  Many friends and relatives, some of whom came from Wisconsin, enjoyed the candle-lighted ceremony and the reception that followed. I wore a gorgeous white satin wedding gown which my dear friend, Lory loaned me after her wedding, which had taken place two months earlier.

Austin's focus in the Navy was preparing to be an engineer, but when he returned home after the war he made a decision to take advantage of a training program and apprenticeship to become a licensed electrician. He earned enough to pay for our living expenses, but I ran out of money to pay for college tuition after my third semester. I left college and went back to work as a legal secretary. I got a very good job in the largest law firm in Minneapolis, and I worked there for about four years. Most of the legal practice was corporate law, which turned out to be a major education for me. The senior partner for whom I worked was a specialist in creating pension and profit sharing plans for large banks and corporations. I believe these plans were a fairly new development in our society. Austin and I saved all of my earnings in a special fund to pay the down payment on our first home. We did not want to start a family until we had a home. That was hard for me, because I really wanted a baby. We built a nice but modest house in a suburb of Minneapolis, and I worked until I was five months pregnant with my first child, Susan, who was born when I was twenty-four in November, 1952.

After I was married and no longer in my parents' home, my mother softened in her relationship to me. She was no longer abusive to me. Marian went to the University of Minnesota, graduating with a BA in humanities. Following her graduation, she moved to San Francisco, where she lived until her death at age forty-two. Looking back, I think my mother was relieved when her responsibilities as a mother were completed. She turned out to be a caring grandmother for Susan, and later for our son, Grant. She and my father would baby-sit for us, either coming to our home or caring for Susan at their home. It was a healing time in my relationship with my mother.

Susan was a bright and beautiful child, and I was thrilled to be a mother. I expected to have another child in a couple of years; however, I did not get pregnant. After working with my gynecologist, undergoing various tests and trying several therapies to help me conceive, none of which resulted in success, Austin and I became involved with an infertility program at the University of Minnesota. The doctor we were working with recommended that I have an x-ray treatment to my pituitary gland in order to stimulate my hormones. I agreed, though it was a scary procedure to have this enormous x-ray machine focused on my head. I was then thirty years old.

Those years of trying to conceive without success were extremely painful for me. Every pregnant woman I saw brought forth feelings of heartbreak.

Eventually, all the doctors concluded that it was unlikely I would become pregnant again, so we started adoption proceedings. After the long interviewing process, they finally approved us for adoption of an infant. I was ecstatic. We were told the waiting period would probably be two years. After one of those years of waiting, I was stunned to find out I had become pregnant. When I missed my second period, I was overjoyed. I called the adoption agency, and they took us off the waiting list.

Then a tragedy occurred for me. I miscarried. Emotionally, I thought I was going to die. Losing that precious baby was one of the most painful experiences of my life. But a miracle occurred about six weeks later when I conceived again. It was a very difficult pregnancy, with many scary moments when I might have had another miscarriage. I had surgery at six months into the pregnancy to keep my cervix from dilating, but I delivered a healthy baby boy, whom we named Grant, just a few months before Susan's eighth birthday. I felt so blessed to have my family.

I was a stay-at-home mom while my children were young, and it was during those child-rearing years that I was active in peace and civil rights activities. My participation was primarily through the outstanding organization called Women's International League for Peace and Freedom (WILPF), to which I was introduced by my mother-in-law, Viena. Austin's mother died when he was nineteen, so I never met her, but his father married Viena when I was about twenty-five. Viena was on the national board of WILPF, and I learned about many activities that inspired me to become active. I had felt strongly for a long time that war was never a viable solution. Thus, in the 1960s I was involved in many activities and demonstrations opposing the war in Vietnam and promoting disarmament. I traveled to Washington, D.C., two different times for peace related conferences and workshops. Also, I had seen and heard Martin Luther King Jr. at a gathering in St. Paul. It was held on the campus of the university, and all of us sat on blankets on a huge lawn. My friends and I got there early and sat in the front. Dr. King stood just a few feet in front of us. I already embraced nonviolence, and I was deeply inspired by Dr. King. I felt compelled to lend my efforts to help reform the racism and inequality in our society. Later some of my black friends invited me to attend meetings with them at a black women's study group in Minneapolis.

During the early years of our marriage, Austin and I were very active members of our Christian church. Both of us were involved in many committees and projects, and I sang in the church choir. Most of our social friends were also active members of the church.

One Sunday morning, in the midst of winter during the early 1960s, there was such a heavy snowfall that all of the side roads were closed until snow plows could clear them. Since we couldn't drive our car on the streets in order to go to church, Austin and I bundled up our children and we all walked to the Universalist Church, which was six blocks from our home. There were only a few people there with the minister, for many of their members couldn't get to church either. We were warmly greeted and felt very much at home. We went back the next Sunday. I felt in harmony with their philosophy and was excited about the freedom and availability of studying not only Christianity, but also other world religions.

This began a process for me of exploring the possibility of leaving our Christian church and becoming active in the Universalist church. Such a change was very painful for me to contemplate, for I loved our friends at the Christian church. It definitely was a difficult process to reach our decision to leave the Christian Church and become active in the Universalist Church. Austin and I had a meeting with our long-time minister, and after much thought and discussion we agreed it was time to move to the new church. I was thirty-three when we made that decision. However, neither of us were prepared for the response we received from our families and old church friends.

Except for Austin's father and Viena, most of our family members were so shocked and dismayed by our decision that some of them literally walked out of our lives. They truly believed we were deluded and no longer believed in God. This was not true, of course. Their anger, judgment, and renunciation was not only painful for us, but deprived our children of the love and companionship of some of their older family members. Eventually the family members came back to us, but there was a reservation and judgment that never completely faded away. Our closest long-time friends at church severed their ties with us. We had been part of a monthly bridge club for many years. There were eight couples, and we rotated each month between our different homes for a pot luck dinner and an evening of bridge. We were all very close friends, but when Austin and I left the church, the group kicked us out of the bridge club. Later on, I could understand their position, but at the time it felt very painful.

From that difficult experience evolved one of my deepest beliefs, and that is that every person has the right to be free to follow their own path, to seek their own higher truth in the way that feels best to them. No one has the right to interfere with that or to impose their will upon someone else's choices.

I never regretted my choice to join the Universalist Church. We made many new friends, I sang in the excellent church choir, and became involved in some of their social action projects. Grant was still a toddler when we joined the church, and about a year later I was shocked to discover that I was pregnant again. All of my pregnancies and deliveries had been difficult, even though each baby was healthy and perfect. When I became pregnant with Sharon, problems arose again.

My mother set aside her judgments about my leaving the Christian Church and helped me in many ways. I appreciated her help enormously, and it was healing for our relationship. It wasn't until I became an adult and a mother myself that I began to understand what my mother had lived through when she was a child. Since she was orphaned when she was very young, I realized she didn't really know how to be a mother. I had long since forgiven her before I became pregnant with Sharon.

A few months into my pregnancy my mother began to show signs of extreme fatigue. She didn't feel well, but she wouldn't go to see a doctor by herself. Finally my father and I insisted that she be checked out. The doctor suspected leukemia and began transfusions to raise her red blood count level which had dropped to a dangerously low level. My mother spent most of the time in the hospital during my last months before I gave birth to Sharon, and she died just three and one-half weeks after my delivery. I was at her bedside when she died; she was fifty-nine. It was only a few days before her death that the blood tests came back positive for a rare form of leukemia.

It was very hard for me to lose my mother just after giving birth to my new daughter. I felt so torn between mothering my new child and spending time with my dying mother. At the same time, Austin's father and a close uncle were ill and hospitalized, so he was busy making hospital rounds. Friends and neighbors helped in many ways, caring for our two little ones and bringing food. Susan was then eleven years old, and she took on many responsibilities for the family. Far more than was best for her age, but she responded beautifully to the family crisis. It was an extremely challenging period in all of our lives. I was grateful, however, for the sweet connection that occurred between my mother and myself during those last weeks of her life.

About a year after Sharon was born, I began to participate in a church project called the Foreign Student program. This project raised funds to support one foreign student each year for nine months. These students had been accepted by the University of Minnesota, and even though they had been awarded a university scholarship to cover tuition, they still needed financial assistance for housing, food, books, and moderate living expenses in order to take advantage of the university scholarship. The student was provided housing in three different church family homes—one family home per university quarter. Austin and I volunteered to provide a home for three months, and the first student that shared our home was a young woman from Korea named Eulbyong. She was an opera singer and was working on a master's degree in music. I loved music, Susan was gifted musically, played the piano and was playing the violin in the school orchestra. We thought it was a good fit.

Grant, Sharon and Susan

Having Eulbyong live with us was such a positive experience that the next year we had another student live with us. We hosted five students in all, two from Africa, and one each from India and Yugoslavia, in addition to the student from Korea. Three women and two men. Each student was unique in personality, in family and cultural background, and in their chosen career. The students blended beautifully into our home and felt very much like family.

Beatrice from Kenya was one of the students who truly felt like family. Not long after she left our home following her three months with us, she became engaged to be married to a graduate student from Kenya at the university. Her mother in Africa had died when she was very young, and Beatrice asked me to be her mother-of-the-bride at her wedding. Our son, Grant, who was then about six, was the ring bearer. It was a joyous event, held in a university area church. The vast majority of the guests were fellow African students, and our family was warmly included in the gathering.

By far, the student who had the most impact and influence on my life was Prasad. I grew immensely through my association with him. Prasad was born into a family of Untouchables, the lowest caste in India. He had a brilliant mind and learned to read as a child. He was the first one to leave his village and go to the city for an education. He had earned a master's degree in English literature in Hyderabad, but there was no program in that university in which he could get a master's degree in journalism, which was his goal. He wanted to be a journalist, for which the University of Minnesota gave him a scholarship.

Everything was new to Prasad when he arrived to live in our home. He was enormously curious and asked questions constantly. Whatever I did or said, he asked me why I did or said that. He was very respectful and kind; he simply was trying to understand the meaning and reason for my every action. Our lifestyle was so totally different from his living experiences in

31

India. He and I had a great relationship, and there developed a high level of trust between us. In response to his constant questions, I was required to look at the basis for all of my actions. What a revelation. I discovered that most of my responses were out of habit, replays of what I had been taught as a child. Many of them—perhaps most of them—were not something I had thought through and chosen for myself. For example, Prasad could not understand why I said "excuse me" as I reached in front of him to pour coffee in his cup. "You are doing me a favor," he said. "Why do you say excuse me?" I began to pay attention to my actions and responses to nearly everything. It was an amazing period of self-discovery. As a result, I became much more authentic in the way I responded to my feelings and various life situations. I also learned so much from him as he shared stories about his family and growing up years in his village.

While he was living with us, we heard on the television one evening about a tragedy that had occurred in India, about which Prasad felt very deeply. He picked up the telephone and called several other Indian students on the university campus, wanting to be with his fellow countrymen. I happened to be in the same room in our home and watched his anguish as each one of these students rebuffed him. He was such a likable person, but the other students came from upper-class wealthy families. Their caste traditions prevented them from including Prasad in their group at that significant moment. As an American, I could not be a comfort to him in the way a fellow Indian student could, but my deep caring for what he was going through created a bond between us, and I grew from this experience.

Others greatly enriched my life. A neighbor, Paul, who lived a few blocks from our home was a social worker and the youth advisor at the Reform Jewish Temple in Minneapolis. He needed some part-time secretarial help for his work at the Temple. I had a typewriter, and for a couple of years I typed up various letters and reports for him in my home. Not only did I brush up my secretarial skills, I also learned a great deal about Jewish traditions, language, and activities. He and his wife and two children became good friends of our family, and they invited us to some special events in their home and in the Temple. Austin and I invited their family to join our family when we went camping for a weekend in northern Minnesota.

We loved camping and canoeing. They were a special joy for all of us. As a family we went tent camping in state parks. Later on we bought a tent trailer and camped on a beautiful secluded twenty-acre piece of land north of Lake Superior. The Knife river flowed through this property which was given to us by Viena. We also had a tandem bike. Austin put together a seat that fit over the front handle bars for little Sharon to sit in. Then he put a basket on each side of the rear wheel and a pad for Grant to sit on. Grant put  one foot in each basket, which protected his legs from the rear wheel. It was terrific. Many evenings after dinner the four of us rode that bike to a nearby lake, and then rode around the lake on the three and one-half mile bicycle path. The kids loved it, and we all had so much fun. In addition, it kept them occupied so that Austin and I could talk without interruption. We were quite a sight, with all four of us on the bike. Susan was then in her early teens and had her own bike. She chose not to be seen with us.

During and following the period of housing foreign students in our home, I continued my involvement in peace and civil rights activities as I had the time. One of the projects I worked with was a program to desegregate the public schools in Minneapolis shortly after the Supreme Court decision created the mandate in the latter part of the 1960s. A pilot project was developed in the Clinton inner-city elementary school. Children from the all-white school districts could choose to be bused to Clinton School, which had students from white, black, Hispanic, and Native American families. We lived in one of those outlying school districts, and Grant and Sharon were participants in that busing program. I was hired as a school secretary and went back to work.

Our home was located in an essentially all-white neighborhood in South Minneapolis. We were well liked in our neighborhood, and most of our neighbors enjoyed the foreign students who lived with us. But there were a few who were fairly upset about having dark-skinned people from Africa and India living in our midst. Adding to that, Susan, who was then in high school, dated for several weeks a dark-skinned African American boy from another school district. I think that added to the discomfort of those neighbors. This was one of the reasons that I wanted Grant and Sharon to experience a different school environment. Sharon was in first grade and Grant in fifth grade that year.

It was definitely an adjustment for my children, but they appeared to thrive in the new environment. I greatly enjoyed working again, especially in a program that was dear to my heart and with committed, caring adults. However, I could never have anticipated the backlash that would occur in our home neighborhood. It became evident that many of our neighbors had instructed their children not to play with our children. In fact, there were some very cruel words and actions by other children toward our kids. This was painful for all of us. Eventually I learned that the parents of some of the other children in our neighborhood thought that I was doing something to destroy our neighborhood school. This was not true, of course, but their fear of change and the Supreme Court decision fueled their belief. They didn't deal with me directly but instead encouraged their children to ostracize my children. It was so hard on Grant and Sharon, and I felt terrible about causing this painful experience for them. That's when I decided that we had to move out of that all-white neighborhood. Austin was in agreement, and he and I began looking at homes for sale in integrated neighborhoods. We did not find any that felt suitable.

During the year that Grant and Sharon were at Clinton School, I was transferred by the Minneapolis school administration to work as a secretary in another inner-city school, Madison elementary school. This school also had a racially-mixed neighborhood student body, plus a new experimental program called the SLBP program for elementary-age children with special learning and behavior problems. The SLBP students were bused in from school districts all over Minneapolis. I was a secretarial assistant to the social workers for each of those two programs. Everyone welcomed me with open arms, and we all worked together to blend the two programs and provide the services the children needed. It was my first experience with children who had severe emotional problems, and I was very touched by the SLBP teachers. They had such compassion and patience. We all truly cared for each of the children, and it was exciting to witness their progress.

Looking back, those years of church participation and social activism provided many rich experiences that deepened my understanding and allowed an awareness that I would not otherwise have had. Then, in my early forties I read *Man's Search for Meaning* by Viktor Frankl, a psychiatrist and survivor of the Holocaust. I was greatly impacted by his book and began reading other stories of personal transformation as well as other spiritual writings. Completely absorbed, I began to shift my focus from social activism to personal growth. This shift created a little distance between my husband and me. He was and is a fine man, and he cared about me and his children. But we grew somewhat apart, for his interests and activities remained with political and social action activities. He really tried to understand my spiritual yearnings and new awarenesses, but to this day, I don't believe he does. It simply is not his reality. And that's all right.

Early in January, 1971 Austin and I began to meet with many other couples and single adults in the exploration of an intentional extended family community. It began with a family who was interviewed in the newspaper, indicating they wanted to be a part of such a community. Austin and I read the article and decided to call them. At that time there were several "communes" in the Twin City area made up primarily of college students and young adults. However, we were not aware of any group that consisted of families. Within this new group I could talk with several of the adults about my new yearnings and insights, and many of them understood. It was a large group. We met weekly for months, and we had one long weekend retreat together in which we explored in depth all sorts of issues that we knew were basic to a large group intending to live together as one household. Over several months, many of the original group participants decided to leave for various reasons, but there remained a beautiful core group of families and single people who were very compatible and excited about pursuing this new community.

By June, just six months after our first meeting, our group had secured a two-year rental lease for a large three-story house on the outskirts of the University of Minnesota campus. It was owned by a fraternity that  was no longer active. Five family units moved in together later that month. This included three complete family units of mother, father, and children; one divorced man and his three young sons; and one single woman. There were nineteen of us in all—eight adults and eleven children ranging in ages from two to sixteen. My husband, our two youngest children, Grant and Sharon, and I were one of the three families. Our older daughter, Susan, was living with a friend in an apartment near the campus of the university at that time. Austin and I easily sold our house. All of the families came from different religious backgrounds. We named it the Castle Community because the younger children thought our new house looked like a castle, and they always referred to it that way.

It was an extraordinary process of combining our respective household goods and furniture. Each person and family chose what they wanted to keep from their individual homes and bring to our new community home. It was fun to then arrange our combined furniture and accessories in the common areas like the living room, dining room, den/music room, and kitchen. Fortunately, we had a very large house, and we created many private bedroom spaces. Our many months of intensive discussion and planning served us well, for we had all come to know and trust each other to a remarkable degree. However, it became evident right away that some creative structure was required to provide for needs such as meal preparation, grocery shopping, kitchen clean-up, and house cleaning. We really enjoyed the whole process. Even though it was a lot of work, and we had some disagreements, we had fun.

The structure that evolved was created by one of the young fathers and a high school girl from another family. They got in a huddle early on and designed an ingenious system that worked extremely well. Everybody in the extended family was divided into three groups. We called them "teams." Each team had two or three adults, some teenagers, and the younger children. The teams stayed together for three weeks. For one week one of the teams was in charge of cooking dinner Monday through Saturday evenings and breakfast on Saturday and Sunday mornings. The next week the same team was responsible for setting and clearing the dining room tables, washing the dishes, and cleaning up the kitchen. The third week the team was responsible for housecleaning all of the common areas in the house, which included the kitchen, pantry, dining room, living room, den, halls, and so forth. After the three-week period, all new teams were created. Usually there was not a husband and wife on the same team, and the teens and children from different families were interspersed among the teams.

It was a brilliant system. We had a family meeting every week, usually on a Thursday night. That night was sacred to the community, and no one missed the meeting unless there was an urgent reason for a person not to attend. We rotated the leadership of the family meetings among adults and teens and put together an agenda in advance. Any family member could put an item for discussion on the agenda. We made all decisions by consensual agreement.

During the weekly family meeting, the three teams gathered separately and organized their work agenda for the following week. The cooking team (or crew) planned the menus for the following week, making out a list of ingredients which would be required to prepare the meals. Someone was responsible to see that the grocery shopping was accomplished. A special calendar was used to list the menus for the week, and the names of the two team members who were in charge of the cooking for each meal were written down. All team members were expected to show up and be present to help with the preparation of the meal. Everybody—adults and children alike—were responsible to their team. If a person couldn't be present for some reason, it was their job to inform the team members in advance. I especially enjoyed the cooking assignment. There were many creative cooks in our extended family, and I had fun learning to cook new dishes, with different seasonings and varied menus.

The team assigned to dining room set-up for dinner and kitchen clean-up would fill out their calendar and post it, and they worked together to divide up the responsibilities. The cleaning crew had their own list, and each person wrote down what they would be responsible for during the week. It was that team's responsibility to see that the scrubbing, dusting, and vacuuming were accomplished each week.

This three-week system created a beautiful working relationship among team members. It developed a strong feeling of family and community, and we all got to know the other family members as we worked with each of them in the different teams. It was a new experience for most of the kids to be supervised by and responsible to other adults besides their parents. Some close and caring bonds were established. Many of the kids began cooking far more often than they had in their nuclear families, and their creativity and enthusiasm were inspiring. Grant really blossomed in the kitchen, and he grew up to be a great cook.

One of the couples owned a used Cadillac hearse, and it became a "family" vehicle. They had put in more seats, and it was very comfortable for a large group of people. We had some wonderful outings in that hearse. One of the first summers my children, Grant and Sharon, and I took a long trip with the family who owned the hearse. We drove to the West Coast and halfway up the east coast of Vancouver Island, camping along the way. We came back through Canada. It was a fabulous trip. At Christmas time many of us would climb into the hearse and drive to a tree farm, where we would select a tree and cut it. We would tie the tree on top of the hearse, and when we got home we would set up the tree. Everybody contributed their decorations, and we'd drink hot apple cider and eat cookies while we put up the decorations. The tree was always gorgeous after it was decorated. We also shared our various holiday traditions and special foods. We celebrated all holidays and birthdays, and they were always festive. We had lots of fun.

Many of the Castle members were musical. We had two pianos, around which children and adults would often gather before dinner to sing while we waited for dinner to be served. I especially loved the music that we shared. Many of us also attended concerts together in the Twin Cities.

A long in-depth book could easily be written about the continuing extraordinary years in our extended family community, but that is not the purpose of this story. I must say that the first couple of years in community created an incredible period of personal growth for each of us. We discovered that as we became more inter-dependent as a group, each of us individually became more independent. Previously, that would have seemed to be a paradox to us.

For me personally, it was exhilarating. I felt as if I had been wanting this for a long time. Yet, as I plumbed my own depths within this group of caring adults, it became so evident to me that most of the other adults knew and understood who I was much more clearly than did my husband of more than twenty years. That was a shocking revelation to me. At the same time, the deep knowing that I had some kind of mission to fulfill continued to grow stronger. I longed to be free to follow my path, but I couldn't bear the thought of asking my husband to leave the community, depriving my children of their father's presence. I was in anguish and did not know what to do.

A very insightful counselor assisted me to work through my feelings and all the issues I had to face. Eventually I concluded that I must separate from Austin. He asked that I not proceed with a divorce right away, and I agreed. I moved out of our joint bedroom and moved into another vacant bedroom in a different part of our large house. Austin and I also sought couples counseling, and a few months later I decided to proceed with the divorce. We went through the entire divorce process while living in our community. All of the other community members loved each of us for who we were, and no one took sides. We were each supported and cared for, as were our children. It may have been the most gentle way a couple could go through the experience of separation and divorce. It was not easy, however; divorce never is. It was a painful process.

During the second year when I worked at Madison school and we lived in the Castle Community, I was asked by the school administration to work in the office one day a week at another inner-city elementary school named Adams. It was the oldest elementary school in Minneapolis. But later that year the school administration decided to close Adams, and the staff of teachers, social workers, and custodians all had to find positions in other schools. Each of them were experiencing fear about receiving a transfer to another school and sadness about leaving Adams. I was astonished when almost all of the staff at one time or another came into the office and talked with me openly about their feelings. Somehow they felt safe to share their feelings with this new part-time secretary.

One day in the spring, when I was having lunch in the lunchroom with the teachers at Adams School, the telephone rang with a call for me. I put down my sandwich and went into another room to take the call. The man calling me identified himself as a doctor in San Francisco. He asked me if I was sitting down. "No," I said, and he kindly suggested that I do so. He told me my sister, Marian, had just died. She had attempted suicide a week before by taking an overdose of pills. Her body apparently had rejected the pills; she vomited a portion of them and then passed out on the floor, where she was not found for two or three days. She was taken to the hospital immediately, but by that time she was very dehydrated and her kidneys severely damaged. She resumed consciousness but asked the doctor not to call me. He said Marian knew she was dying, which was what she wanted, and she also knew that I would fly out immediately to be with her. She did not want that, so she made the doctor promise that he would not call me until after her death. I later thanked him for honoring Marian's request, even though it was so painful for me.

He gave me his name along with the name and phone number of the hospital, then suggested that it might be best if I went home and called him from there for other details. Marian had given the doctor my home phone number, and he had called the Castle, where Jerry, who was one of the young fathers in the community, had given him my school phone number. Jerry had told the doctor that he would go and pick me up immediately but would wait for my call. I was terribly shaken, but when I called Jerry I told him I could drive the short distance home. I just wanted him to be there when I arrived. By the time I got home, Jerry had called all the other Castle adults. All but one of them was able to come home fairly soon to assist me. When I called Marian's doctor back after I got home, it was clear that I needed to fly to San Francisco as soon as possible.

Next I called my Dad. He had remarried a couple years after my mother's death, and at that time he and his wife lived in Florida. He had heart trouble and was not well enough to travel. Austin happened to be home at that time, taking some vacation time to work on his income tax. None of the other adults were in a position to leave their respective jobs and go to San Francisco with me, but Austin said he would go. (I had separated from him and moved to my new bedroom only a few weeks before.) I will always be grateful to him for that gesture, even though it was hard for both of us.

Everybody pitched in immediately to help me get ready to leave. I was surrounded with loving, caring people. One packed my bags. Another one called and canceled my appointments for the next week, while I made my plane and hotel reservations and talked with Marian's doctor, co-workers, and others in San Francisco. Austin made a trip to our bank to retrieve Marian's personal information and instructions, which we had stored in our safety deposit box. Still another one took Austin and me to the airport. I think we boarded the plane by six o'clock that evening.

When Grant and Sharon came home from school a little after three o'clock, I told them their Aunt Marian had died, and I was leaving shortly to fly to San Francisco. Grant asked me how Marian had died, and I told him gently but honestly. One of the women in our community, whose father had taken his own life many years before, sat down with us to share that experience with my children. I felt so comforted that my kids would be in safe and caring hands while I was gone.

Finally, when I was on my way to California, the tears came. I think I cried throughout most of the flight. It was only four months before Marian's death that my beloved Grandma Jo, who was then in her nineties, had died from terminal cancer just before Christmas. She had moved back to Minneapolis from California and lived the last few years of her life in the Masonic Home. I visited her often, and it was a deep loss in my life when she passed on. And now I had lost my sister as well.

It was a very hard, painful week in California, taking care of all the necessary arrangements. But I was continually amazed at the kindness extended toward me. Several people made major adjustments in their schedules in order that I could accomplish everything that needed to be done in just one week. Marian had never been married. As I sorted through her personal papers and belongings, I discovered notes to me that indicated she had been planning to take her life for some time. I learned in a phone conversation with a police officer that when the police had been called to her apartment, they found a letter written by Marian to me with instructions and information about what she wanted done. They took the letter to police headquarters and were not allowed to release it to me at that time because of some regulation. They did, however, mail it to me about a month later. It would have been helpful to have that letter while I was making all the final arrangements, but Marian's instruction sheet, which I had kept in our safety deposit box, provided me with the facts I needed.

It was Marian's deepest sorrow to know that she could not shield me from this process. She would have spared me that task if she could. She had been counseling with a psychiatrist for an extended period, trying to resolve and to heal the many painful conflicts and wounding from her childhood. I talked at length by phone with her psychiatrist while I was in San Francisco and felt comforted in knowing she had tried so hard. I deeply wished that Marian and I had been able to talk more openly with each other about our childhood traumas. After she left Minnesota, it never felt right to bring it up with her when we were together. Perhaps neither of us was ready. It was several years after her death before I was able to open myself fully and find healing for my wounding.

Within the one-week period I was in San Francisco, I took care of all her financial arrangements and packed up all her personal belongings. Some of them I boxed and mailed to my home at the Castle. The rest I gave to her neighbors or left for the Salvation Army to pick up. It was an arduous task.

During that week I called home to the Castle every night, which the Castle adults had asked me to do. There was an intercom system in that former fraternity house, so when I called, the person who answered immediately went on the intercom and the message went out all over the house that I was on the phone. (This was long before cell phones were invented.) I think there were about five telephones in the house, so I could share with many of my family members at the same time. I always talked with Grant and Sharon. The love and support of my family community was unbelievably nurturing and kept me going that week.

This was not the first time I had dealt with suicide. My mother had attempted and failed in her suicide attempt about a year before she developed the symptoms of leukemia. That was about eight years before Marian's death. She, as Marian, desperately wanted to leave this life, and when her suicide attempt with pills didn't work, I think she unconsciously created the life-threatening disease of leukemia instead. My father could not understand either my mother's or my sister's desire for suicide. Neither he nor I ever had that inclination. He instructed me not to tell any of our relatives the whole truth about Marian's suicide. He told all the family members that Marian died of kidney failure, which was, in fact, true, but the cause of the kidney failure was never revealed. Many years later my father and I were able to talk about this with great understanding and compassion between us. My father passed away a few years later after having had several heart attacks in the preceding ten years. He was sixty-nine. He and I had a good relationship and had some beautiful conversations while he was in the hospital prior to his death.

Through all of that week, and after I returned home, I felt peaceful about Marian's decision to take her life. I felt the pain of her anguish and my loss very deeply, but it didn't feel wrong to me that she chose to end her life, and I felt no judgment. That greatly surprised me; I didn't understand it at all. I had always heard that committing suicide was not an acceptable option. It was nearly fifteen years later that I was to learn the reason for this and to find validation for my intuitive knowing.

The week following my return home to Minneapolis I went back to work at the two schools. I had a large backlog of work that needed to be accomplished in each location. I was extremely tired. But everyone was very kind. Each evening I was comforted by ones in the community and encouraged to process the experience as I felt the need and desire. The whole experience was truly extraordinary.

I need to now back up a year in my story in relation to school experiences. When all of us in the Castle Community moved into the big house the year before, in 1971, Grant and Sharon had to change schools once again. The Castle was in a school district that provided three options for elementary school. Austin and I decided that the open school would be the best choice for Sharon. There was structure, although it was not as rigid as a traditional school, and it was easy walking distance for her from home. Grant and two of the other Castle boys chose to attend a new Free School program which had just been developed as part of the Minneapolis Public School system. It was located right across a large parking lot from our house, and Grant liked it very much. I continued working at Madison School. After that first year of the Free School, the Minneapolis school administration determined that they needed a secretary. I applied and was hired. It was a public school with kindergarten through twelfth grade, the first of its kind in Minneapolis.

The office was in chaos when I began working there, for the school had expanded its program from seventy-five students the first year to 150 students that second year. There was no secretary the first year, and the teachers had just boxed up and moved all of the school records into a new room designated as the office. In addition, there was a new principal, a well-qualified man from the East Coast. However, he was new to the city and had no experience with the school administration in Minneapolis. It was a challenge for everybody on the staff. Sorting out all of those school records and establishing a workable office system that met the main school administration's requirements was a daunting task. The stress level was high, but the principal and all of the teachers were exceedingly helpful and supportive. We really worked well together as a team, which was necessary since the student body had doubled and the seventy-five new students had to be integrated into the program.

It became my responsibility to be the liaison between our school staff and the Minneapolis public school administration. Several times over the course of that year I drove to the main office for a meeting with some of their personnel. We all wanted this experimental program to succeed, but there were strict accounting policies with which we had to comply. I could not report our data in the usual format used by other schools because our students did not fall into the traditional categories such as Mrs. Jones, grade one, room 101. Our students were divided into small groups. Each group had a teacher who was an advisor and involved children of different ages and grade levels. Eventually we worked out a system of accounting that met the administration requirements. I worked hard to set up a reporting system that our teachers would respond to and that would provide me with the data I needed. At the same time, our new school principal asked me to be an advisor to two of the school families. I was quite thrilled that he thought I was qualified for that responsibility, and it was a great experience for me and for the families.

During that year at the Free School, I began to notice that most of the teachers, and occasionally the principal, would come in to the office to talk to me about some troubling situation in their personal lives. Eventually some of the teachers dubbed me the unofficial school psychiatrist. They told me I was a good, compassionate listener, and they greatly encouraged me to go back to school and get an education that would prepare me to be a professional counselor. I thought about that a lot and decided to enter the University of Minnesota the following September on a part-time basis.

It was also during that year that I made the painful decision to start divorce proceedings. It took months and the process was stressful, culminating with a court hearing and a final divorce decree in mid-April, shortly after my forty-fifth birthday. That was quite a year in my life.

At that point the Castle Community's two-year rental lease was expiring, and the fraternity informed us that they would be selling the house and therefore would not renew our lease. We could not afford to buy that house, but we decided as a community we did want to jointly buy a large house. We could not find the right house in Minneapolis, but an amazing orchestration of events connected us with a huge, beautiful home in St. Paul. It was right next door to the Governor's mansion. Several of us went to look at it, loved it, and made an offer, which was accepted. Two couples, two single adults, and I each invested $5,000 for a down payment of $25,000. This was a substantial down payment back in 1973. A friend of the community, an attorney named Chet, created the legal entity of a housing cooperative, to which we all belonged. The co-op actually purchased the property, and that was to be our home for the next five years.

By that time, Austin chose to move out of the community into his own apartment in Minneapolis. I was given custody, so Grant, Sharon, and I continued to be part of the Castle Community. Since Austin spent time with our children regularly, he and I saw each other fairly often. Sometimes it was difficult for me, but we have remained friends throughout all these years. I am grateful to him for the consistent caring he has shown to our children and to me.

Not long before the divorce was final, a friend in the peace movement called me. The landmark decision, Roe v. Wade, had just been handed down by the Supreme Court, making abortion legal. Several people were in the process of putting together the first abortion clinic in Minnesota, and I was asked to join with them and be part of the staff as a counselor. I protested that I had no professional training or experience, but they felt I had other qualities that were more important than a degree. It would be an experiment for all of us, since it would be the first of its kind in Minnesota, and there was no one to train us.

This began a most remarkable chapter in my life. I did not have strong feelings about abortion, for I fortunately had never had an unwanted pregnancy and had never had to face that very difficult decision. But I did have strong feelings that every woman has a right to choose what is best for her life. Our staff was committed to providing a very professional clinic in which a woman would be given excellent medical care and also be treated with dignity as a whole person, and not just as a person with a medical problem. An existing group of three Obstetrics and Gynecology doctors in Minneapolis were committed to providing the medical services—a courageous step for these doctors.

I continued working at the Free School long enough to prepare the data needed for the year-end reports and to help an assistant secretary get ready to take over my job. At the same time, all of us in the Castle Community were packing and preparing for our move to the mansion in St. Paul in the latter part of June. This was an intense period for me. I was excited about my new job at the clinic and about our community moving to this gorgeous new home. However, I was still healing from the divorce process and the loss of my sister and grandmother who had passed away the previous year. I feel very blessed by all the kindness and understanding I received from many friends and Castle family members. Looking back, I think the necessity of preparing for the move to our new home and for my new job at the clinic provided an all-consuming focus that helped me make the transition.

Chapter 3
Women's Clinic—University—Women's Shelter

On May 1, 1973, the Women's Clinic opened in a suburb of Minneapolis. Our new staff had prepared well, and we worked well together. There was never any judgment of a person's behavior or their choice to have an abortion. There was great caring and compassion exhibited toward each woman who came to the clinic, and also between staff members and doctors. Once the needs and responses of the women patients became evident, we adjusted our services.

Often protesters who were opposed to abortion demonstrated outside the building where the clinic was located. Sometimes it became ugly when the protesters tried to prevent people from entering the building, but no one was injured. All of us on the staff were committed to keeping this service available to women who chose it and to improving our services as we became aware of the needs.

Working at the clinic was an incredible experience for me. My heart was so touched by the stories each woman told during our individual counseling sessions prior to the actual abortion procedure. No woman I ever counseled found abortion to be an easy decision. Each one anguished over this situation in her life and told me it was the hardest thing she ever had to do. I worked with women of all ages. They were from every race, social, and economic background; they were professional people, including minister's and judge's wives, single women, and couples with very low incomes.

We counselors went with each of our clients to the medical room and stood by her as she had the abortion. For each woman I counseled I would hold her hand and be a support for her physically and emotionally. Sometimes she was weeping, and I comforted her so that she could try to relax and thus allow the doctor to more easily perform the procedure. It was never easy, but it was rewarding for all of us on the staff. Following the procedure, the woman would be taken to the recovery room for an hour or two. She was cared for by a nurse, given something to eat and drink, and then discharged when she was stable and ready to go home. We provided information to them about contraceptive methods and support services that were available in the cities to help meet their other needs, and they appreciated all of us on the staff.

I usually worked with three women patients each day. I discovered that I was a natural for this work. I developed rapport with each woman quickly. They trusted me and felt my compassion.

One of the serious problems that became evident in our counseling sessions was that many of the women were being physically, mentally, and emotionally battered by their husband, partner, father, brother, or other family member or friend, and they had no place to go. There were no shelters available at that time.

While I was working at the clinic I began to be aware of a warmth and vibration that would come into my hands at times. I did not know what caused it to occur, but as time went on, some of the "family" members of our Castle Community would comment on it when I would massage them or touch them when they were ill or in pain. I mentioned this to a couple of the counselors at the clinic, and fairly soon different staff members began asking me to put my hands on them when they were having pain. All of them reported to me that the pain went away. I had never heard of spiritual healing at that point and had never met or experienced a healer, so I had no awareness of what was going on. This eventually would lead to my studying with a Reiki master named Ethel Lombardi. I will explore this in depth a little later in my story.

A few months after the clinic opened, I started my studies at the University of Minnesota. I carried about eight credits each quarter, in addition to working about twenty hours per week at the clinic. I was in an outstanding small program called Human Services in the General College at the University. There were many students in the program that were already working, as I was, in some form of human services. These included counselors in various agencies, corrections officers, and the like. Most of us were in our thirties or forties, had a variety of work experiences, and wanted to get a credential or degree, in addition to other forms of university knowledge and training.

In addition to the classroom courses, which included interviewing and counseling techniques, I also had three different internships. I worked in a state mental hospital, in a program for chemical dependency treatment, and in a newly-formed center comprised of two psychiatrists and several counselors and mental health practitioners. These internships were invaluable experiences for me. I discovered that I learn more easily in a working environment than in a classroom setting. Fortunately in this university program I could relate the classroom techniques to my work at the clinic and to each internship setting. I also learned that I definitely thrive on variety.

My internship with the chemical dependency treatment program was an extraordinary experience for me. The first couple of weeks I spent all day long in the residential portion of the treatment program, getting acquainted with the participants who were just beginning their treatment. Hearing their stories, their aspirations, and witnessing their struggles made a deep impression upon me. I was humbled to hear such honesty and determination to start facing the consequences of their behavior.

Another intern in the program was a man who was a recovering alcoholic. He had gone through treatment programs several times before he succeeded in his recovery, and was at that time the head counselor at another very well-known chemical dependency treatment center. We often ate lunch together and shared our responses to the sessions. It was helpful to both of us because we came from such different life experiences. I had never had an alcohol problem, nor did anyone in my family. He shared with me the incredible struggle he had gone through in his life with alcohol abuse, and the heartbreak it had caused between him and his wife. He said my observations were valuable to his understanding, and I was greatly enriched by both his personal story and observations of the program. Toward the end of the quarter, he invited me to spend a day at his treatment center, which was another valuable experience.

I came away from those three months with a whole new understanding about the addictions that grip so many people in our society, and the really heroic efforts required to heal themselves and their relationships with their families and friends. I witnessed enormous courage. I deeply honor and respect all those who have chosen to release their dependencies and who have gone through the arduous process of healing, and living their lives without the substances to which they were formerly addicted.

One of the other students in this Human Services program at the university, a woman named Mary, was a corrections officer at the state women's prison, which was in an outlying area about twenty miles from Minneapolis. She had been interested in starting a small support group in the prison but felt she needed a co-leader with some group skills. She asked me if I would consider leading this group with her once a week in the afternoon for ten weeks, and I enthusiastically agreed to do so. She then convinced the warden to allocate a small fund with which to pay me a small stipend for my time and travel expenses.

I had never been in a prison before, so I was shocked to be checked in and have my purse and coat all locked up in a special room. Mary met me and took me to the room where we would hold the group sessions. She had selected five women whom she felt would participate and benefit from the group experience. All of them had consented. When the five women were all in the room with Mary and me, a prison employee locked the door on the outside, with us inside. It was an eerie feeling, but I was not afraid. My recollection is that the women prisoners were mostly in their thirties and forties. Mary introduced me, and both of us shared some of our life experiences so that these women could get acquainted with us, even though they already knew Mary.

I could tell very shortly that the women prisoners were not going to just start talking about themselves, as I had experienced in other support group situations. There was a rather uncomfortable silence. Then I had the inspiration to suggest that we each tell every woman in the room one thing we liked about her. I started with Mary, whom I knew, and then went around the room. I did not know them yet, but I remember saying to one of them, "I like the way you fix your hair." The other women nodded and agreed. "Really?" the woman said, shocked. To someone else who had seemed to be a bit more open to all of this, I said I liked her smile. Again, the others agreed.

There was an amazing shift in the energy of the group. Mary complimented each woman in turn, and again the other women nodded. Slowly the women prisoners took turns, some being more shy than others, but to each compliment the woman seemed to be very touched, and usually surprised. I wondered how long it had been since any of them had felt any validation for herself. Before the two-hour group session ended, a couple of the women did talk a little hesitantly about their fears for their family members and their parole. I left feeling touched by what happened.

The following week, the day before the next scheduled group session at the prison Mary called me at the women's clinic. She told me she would not be able to be there for the group because she needed to fly to California. One of the prison inmates had escaped and then been located and taken into custody there. Mary needed to go to California and bring her back to the prison but wouldn't arrive in time for the group session. She told me she had talked to the five women in the group, and they wanted me to come anyway to hold the group session. She asked me if I was willing to do it alone. Without hesitation, I said, "Yes, of course I will, if they want it." So we agreed, and she said she would tell the other women participants before she left for California. After our phone conversation ended, I suddenly remembered that I would be locked in that room with five women who were all in prison for some kind of physical crime or murder. I definitely felt some apprehension, but I also felt it was right for me to go.

The next day after the usual procedure to check me in, I was taken to the group room. The five others were already there. They greeted me rather shyly, and I didn't feel any animosity from any of them. Rather, a couple of them began to talk about aspects of their lives. The time seemed to go by quickly, and I was surprised when a guard told us the group time was finished. They asked me if I would come back the next week, and I said with a smile that I would. I think they trusted me at that point. My heart sang all the way as I drove home.

The next week Mary was there with me, and the women opened up still more freely. Over the remainder of those ten weeks I learned a great deal about each woman. Many of their stories were horrendous, and I often thought, "There, but for the grace of God, go I." With the background of abuse in each woman's history, I could easily understand how these crimes could have taken place. I told them about the abuse I suffered as I was growing up. Many of the women had children at home, and they anguished about their separation from them. I think their biggest fear was going before the parole board, and we helped them prepare for that.

One of the issues that came up in the group was unwanted pregnancies. I learned that most of them knew very little, if anything, about contraception. I asked them if they wanted me to teach them what I knew, and they were all enthusiastic. In fact, they said they wanted me to share this information at a meeting for all the inmates, not just for our small group. Mary and the warden set up a time for me to stay after one of the group sessions, have dinner with the inmates, and then teach them about contraception. It was a pretty amazing happening. I was taken with them to the dining hall where we ate. Afterwards, we were all taken to a different building and locked in again. I had brought with me many of the contraceptive devices and materials about how pregnancy occurs that we used in small group teaching sessions at the clinic. I was astonished at how little most of the women prisoners knew about their bodies and pregnancies. They were so excited to get this information and thanked me profusely before I left.

When the ten-week program was completed, the prison board would not extend the small stipend they paid me. But I had other obligations at that point, and Mary felt confident about continuing to lead the group herself. I felt some sadness when I left them for the last time, although I also felt grateful for that incredible experience and my own growth in those ten weeks.

Shortly after that, one of my friends on the staff at the clinic was preparing to go to the hospital for a laparascopic tubal ligation, which would be performed by one of our clinic doctors. I was considering the possibility of having a tubal ligation myself and, at my request, my friend and the doctor gave me permission to be present in the operating room while he performed the procedure on her. As directed, I arrived at the hospital very early in the morning. I was given a sterile gown to wear, coverings for my shoes, head, hands, and face, so I could be present while my friend was being prepped and the anesthetic was administered. The head operating room nurse was upset about my presence because I was not medically trained, and she attempted to prevent my presence in the OR. However, since the doctor and the patient approved it, she reluctantly acquiesced.

During the procedure, after the doctor had made the abdominal incision, he asked me if I would like to look through the laparascope into the abdominal cavity of my friend. The incision was very small, and right by the navel. At the other end of the laparascope there was an incredible magnifying device. When I looked through it, I was astounded. It was like looking through a periscope into her abdomen. I could see all of her organs—liver, stomach, intestines, uterus, and so on. Each organ was a different color, and all were vibrant and pulsing with energy. I was absolutely in awe of the magnificence of our bodies. That vision is indelibly etched in my memory. A few weeks later, the same doctor performed the identical surgery on me. I think there were two or three of our clinic counselors who observed my surgery in the hospital, and the doctor allowed them to view my abdominal cavity as well.

While in the university program, I was always looking for resources for the women who came to the clinic for abortions and who were being battered. I learned about a small task force of women who were trying to open up a shelter in St. Paul for battered women and their children. I arranged to meet with Sharon Rice Vaughn, who was the primary coordinator for this group, and I was very excited about their plans. The group was able to open the doors of their new shelter in October 1974, which they called Women's Advocates. As far as we knew, it was the first shelter for battered women in the United States. At last there was a resource for the battered women who came to the clinic.

Late December1974, while I was at work at the clinic, I was called into the administrator's office and told that I was being terminated from my job because of a need for a staff cutback. Two other abortion clinics had opened in the Twin Cities during the past few months and our client load was not as large as it had been previously, so I felt certain that this cutback would need to occur. However, I was stunned that I was one of the counselors who was terminated because I had been training the new counselors for a long time and was one of the original staff from two and one-half years ago. The new administrator also knew that I was leaving after work that day and flying to Philadelphia for a week's vacation. I was told that this was my last day at the clinic and that I should take everything that belonged to me when I left that day. When I told the other clinic staff members what had happened, they all went into a panic about the security of their own jobs. I was devastated, not only by the news but by the unfeeling way in which I was told. I left for Philadelphia in shock and panic about how I was going to support myself and my two youngest children, Grant and Sharon. Only later did I realize that it was a blessing in disguise. I had not yet learned that there are no accidents and that a purpose is served in every experience.

When I returned from Philadelphia I began the process of applying for and collecting temporary unemployment checks. It was a humbling experience, for I had never been terminated from a job, school, or any situation. At that time we had to go in person to the downtown office and stand in line for our check. There I met many people, including professional people, who were going through a similar experience, so I didn't feel as alone and rejected.

At our next family meeting in the Castle Community, someone suggested and all agreed that my monthly contribution to the food and maintenance fund should be cut back until I got another job. They said they would each contribute a little more to cover it. I was stunned and so grateful for their caring and generosity.

Now without a job, I decided to complete the few remaining credits at the university in order to receive my two-year AA degree. The University of Minnesota administration office refused to accept some of my credits from Macalester College, which they initially told me would be applied toward my degree. They insisted that I needed eight more credits. I argued a strong case, but in the end their decision prevailed. Again, this was an unrecognized blessing.

I did not want to sit in the class room for any more classes, so I contacted the newly-opened Women's Advocates shelter and asked if they would be interested in my doing an in-depth independent study at the shelter on "Women in Crisis." I would work in the shelter for three months in whatever capacity I was needed, for however many hours I was needed without pay. I was enthusiastically welcomed, and thus I began my work with battered women.

Women's Advocates 2007

All of the advocates at the shelter were bright, gifted women, committed to creating a safe haven, a refuge for battered women and their children. However, none of them had as much experience as I had with counseling and group work. It had already become evident that these were important needs. So I created a counselor training program for the advocates to teach them what I had learned. I also started a support group, held one evening each week, to which the women currently staying at the shelter could come. They could continue to attend after they left the shelter, since the group was also open to women in the community who did not need the shelter but were dealing with abuse in their lives. One of the other advocates co-facilitated the group with me. The support group at the shelter still continues all of these many years later.

Even though the house was somewhat dilapidated, it was the most beautiful working environment I had ever been a part of. The shelter staff operated as a collective, making decisions by consensual agreement. There was such a genuine closeness between the staff and the women and children who came to the shelter for safety.

I spent many hours each week listening and counseling with the women residents. It was painful to hear their stories, to witness the bruises and trauma each one had endured. Most of the women brought their children to the shelter and they, too, were traumatized. My heart was deeply touched by all of them. I was overwhelmed at the same time—overwhelmed at the complexity and enormity of interpersonal violence in our society and the extraordinary difficulties women have in extricating themselves from abusive and destructive situations.

The advocates provided many services. One of us accompanied each woman to her appointment with the welfare department so that the shelter would receive payment for her food and shelter. We took her to the hospital if she needed it, to the county attorney's office or to the police if needed, and to any other service she required. Every evening after dinner when the young children had been put to bed, the advocate on duty held a meeting in the living room. Each woman would share what her needs were for the following day, and a schedule was written up for the staff coming in the next morning.

The welfare department and other agencies required identification, such as a birth certificate, marriage certificate, or drivers license. Almost all of the women had fled in a hurry from the battering situation and had no identification with them. Nor did they have other items they needed, such as clothing and toiletries. In order to pick up these needed items, they had to go back home. This was a frightening experience for each woman.

The advocate who accompanied the woman called the police department and arranged for a police escort. The police officer was allowed to stay with us for only ten minutes, but we were always grateful for the protection. Sometimes the batterer was present in the home, but there never was any violence when a police officer accompanied us. We planned ahead and took large heavy-duty garbage bags with us, into which the woman could quickly gather up the personal items she needed. I experienced this traumatic trip with many women.

When the three-month period of the university quarter was coming to completion, I wrote a twenty-two page paper. The last three pages consisted of questions for which none of us had answers. There had not been a single book published in the United States about battered women in 1975.

After I received my AA degree in Human Services from the University of Minnesota, some of my friends urged me to continue and get a master's degree in counseling. But I knew at a deep level that this was not to be my path. I had the strong feeling that what I needed to do was find a way to "remember" what I already knew from some other level of knowing. I did not understand this intellectually, but I felt confident that I could do what I wanted to do without the credential the university could provide. Another critical consideration was my concern that if I continued academic studies at the university, I might lose touch with the intuitive "knowing" that had already developed. Even though I am now enormously grateful for the knowledge I received and the enriching experiences I was privileged to have in the Human Services program, then I felt almost constantly on guard in protecting my intuitive abilities.

Meanwhile, enough additional funds had been provided to allow the shelter to hire another staff person. I applied for the job, along with a large number of other women, and was fortunate to be selected to join the staff. I worked at the shelter for four and one-half years, facilitating ongoing weekly support groups and providing all kinds of counseling and advocacy services. It was a powerful experience for me, and I grew enormously in my own self-awareness.

Soon after I started working at the shelter, we advocates discovered that many of the women residents had a history of incest. The staff agreed that we needed some training, and we all took a workshop in Minneapolis for this purpose. In the process of my participation in this course, I remembered scenes from my young adolescence of three incidents of incest from my father. As so many others have done, I had buried those memories deep within me out of shame and fear that my mother would somehow find out and blame me. I learned during the course that this was a typical response. It was a painful process to remember those experiences, but I was very grateful for the clearing that occurred. Even though I had not previously remembered those incidents consciously, I felt as though something very important had been lifted and released.

As I mentioned earlier in this chapter, it was during the years I worked at the abortion clinic that I became aware of the warmth and energy that was coming through my hands, which other people told me helped them to release pain and feel better. This continued as I worked at the shelter, and sometimes I would put my hands on the women residents or staff if they were open to my touching them, and when I felt the intuitive sense I should do this, or if one of the women requested it.

Grant, Sharon, and I were living in the Castle Community at that time in the large mansion in St. Paul. Over the years, from time to time, we members invited several gifted people from other parts of the country to come and stay with us for a few days or weeks. One of them was a professional massage therapist from California, from whom I learned how to give a massage. I loved giving a massage to others and receiving it myself. As the warmth and energy came through my hands automatically while I was giving the massage, there were times when the healing was so dramatic that I could not deny that something profound was happening. It was clear that I wasn't doing it—it was being done through me. I wanted to understand what was happening, but I didn't know who to talk to.

Shortly after that, in 1977, one of the men in our Castle Community attended an introductory session given by a Reiki master named Ethel Lombardi who had come to the Twin Cities from Chicago. He volunteered to be the person on whom Ethel demonstrated the Reiki spiritual healing technique. That evening, after having had that experience, he told me he wasn't sure what Ethel was doing, but it felt like what happened when I put my hands on him. He greatly encouraged me to take the Reiki course from Ethel and helped me pay for the tuition. Reiki is a natural or spiritual healing and growth system founded by Dr. Mikao Usui in the late nineteenth century. At a first-degree class in Reiki, the Reiki master attunes the student to a limitless source of spiritual or divine healing energy. More information about Reiki is given at the end of this book.

So in November 1977, I began my Reiki studies with Ethel. At that time I believe Ethel was one of only five Reiki masters in this country. (Now there are thousands of Reiki masters around the world.) At last I began to have an understanding about this energy and how to work with it. Furthermore, I had other people in my life who understood and worked with energy. After the first class, Reiki I, several of us from that class began meeting once a week to practice on each other. It was like a support group for me, and within that group I fully embraced and allowed the energy to flow through me. About three months later I took the Reiki II class. In this class I learned how to send long-distance healings, which are also called "absent healings."

It was during those years at the Castle that I was introduced to various practices and therapies that were totally new to me. I learned to meditate. I took yoga and tai' chi classes, and I began to practice them regularly. I also had my body rolfed. Rolfing is deep tissue body work, much deeper than massage. Rolfing sessions release the blockages caused by many old physical injuries and traumas. These sessions were extremely helpful to me. I worked with bioenergetics and biofeedback, and participated in innumerable spiritual workshops, classes, and conferences around the country. I loved it all. It was the beginning of my spiritual awakening.

As my work at the shelter continued, there were times when a woman resident with whom I had been counseling would leave the shelter and ask me if she could continue to come to me for counseling. The mansion where our community lived was only about a mile from the shelter, so I invited each woman who made that request to come to my home where we could have private and uninterrupted time together. I also had friends who began to ask me to give them a massage. I set up a massage table and two comfortable chairs for counseling in an unused room at the Castle. That was the beginning of my private practice in massage, healing, and counseling.

One of the other special guests invited to the Castle was a woman from the East Coast who was very intuitive and a trained spiritual counselor. In my first session with her, I experienced a spontaneous remembering of a past life in which I was a Native American woman. It was a vivid recall—a memory that was so real I could not deny it. That opened another door for me, which called forth memories of other lives. Sometimes they were facilitated by others, and at other times they occurred spontaneously to me.

While all of this was happening, many changes were occurring within our Castle Community. Several of the early members had left over the five years we lived in the mansion, and new people had joined with us and moved in. Sometimes the reasons for members leaving were happy ones, but more often the reasons were traumatic. At times there were disagreements that we were not as a group able to resolve. Eventually this resulted in a decision to disband the community and sell the house.

Despite the pain and difficulties that existed, my overwhelming response to the seven-year experience in community living is that it was marvelous for me and for my children. Occasionally when someone found out that the community was ending, I would hear that person say that the community was a failure because it had broken up. I never felt that it had failed. It was a glorious experiment that provided remarkable growth, and enormous support and nurturing to the family members. We made lots of mistakes and sometimes hurtful things happened. Some of them I regretted deeply, but I never regretted joining with others to live in community.

We put the big mansion up for sale in 1977. A buyer emerged, and in February 1978, we signed a sale agreement, with the closing date set for May 15. When the closing date arrived, the buyer wouldn't close with us, nor would he release us from the agreement. It became evident he was a crook; he owned an investment company and knew all the real estate games. What followed was a major legal entanglement. Fortunately, our lawyer, Chet, for whom I worked as a secretary one day a week, knew more about the laws governing co-ops than anyone else around, and after months of following the necessary legal procedures, it was resolved by the end of October. We found another buyer the next summer; we completed the sale to him in November, and he happily moved into the mansion.

Chet and I worked hard in this process, and though it was frustrating, I learned a lot. Also, because of the situation, all of the previous adults who owned shares in the Castle co-op had to pull together to deal with the catastrophe. The five extra months gave us time to bring about closure of the community. So it was good. There were deep bonds between most of the Castle people, and I still keep in contact with many of them. We were truly "family" to each other in a very precious way. I am grateful for these relationships and for the rich seven-year experience we had.

The profit I gained from the sale of my shares in the Castle Community allowed me to buy another house, a lovely seventy-year-old three-story house just four blocks from the Castle. I bought it from a good friend. The house had six bedrooms and two and one-half baths, and we lived there for seven years. My oldest daughter, Susan, was then living in New York City, but Grant, Sharon, and I had three of the four bedrooms on the second floor. We usually had two or three others who shared our home with us. It was quite different to be living with a small group in a much smaller house, but there were some positive aspects. I had closer contact with Grant and Sharon, and I learned still another level of independence.

However, I continued to dream about being part of a larger community again some day, and at that time I hoped it would be connected with a holistic health center. The new house was a source of frustration for me at times, as it needed lots of repair and decorating. And there was a totally different dynamic in our small "community" because I owned the house and was ultimately responsible for everything. I truly missed the group participation we enjoyed in the Castle Community.

Not long after we moved into the house I now owned, I attended a workshop in Vermont with two of my close friends. At the workshop I met two other participants who were attempting to form a residential community situation in Vermont with people who were involved in healing and spiritual growth. We kept in contact. Later that year I went back to Vermont to explore with them the possibilities, but the community did not come together. Nor did a community in Colorado materialize with a group I became involved with there. So I continued to try to create a small community in my home with Grant, Sharon, and a couple of others.

In 1980 two close friends connected with the Castle Community invited me to join them and several others for a week-long trip to an island in the Bahamas. I was excited about seeing another culture and being close to the ocean beaches in the winter. We all brought snorkeling equipment with us. My friends drove to Florida, but I flew down and met them at the airport in Miami. While on the island, we all stayed in the large home of a woman who was a friend of one of the members of our group. It was right on the ocean. She cooked for us and drove us around in her vehicle. It was great.

We had many wonderful experiences, but the most memorable for me were the two times we went snorkeling. I was blown away the first time I put my face in the water and saw the thousands of gorgeous tropical fish and the coral reefs. I felt as if I were in another world, viewing this radiant, vibrant life that is not at all visible on the surface of the water. I will always treasure those memories. In a sense, they reminded me of the time a few years earlier when I observed my friend's tubal ligation in the hospital and the doctor allowed me to look through the laparascope at the inside of her abdominal cavity. Once again I was reminded of the extraordinary beauty that is not always easy to observe on this beautiful earth.

When we left the island and arrived at the Miami airport, the others left to drive back to Minnesota. I stayed in a motel overnight, and the next morning I rode the bus to the outskirts of the city where I met a Cuban woman whom I had previously contacted by mail while I was in Minnesota. She was preparing for a caucus, a gathering of Hispanic people in Miami for the following weekend. She was swamped with details, so I helped her type up reports, assemble materials, and get organized to prepare for the event. She invited me to stay in her home.

The participants for the caucus came from around the country and were each involved in some community project in the United States that provided services for Hispanic people. Just before the gathering I had the opportunity to meet many of these wonderful people, and also see the living and working conditions of many of the Cuban refugees in Miami. Much of it was deplorable. During the caucus sessions, many of the participants gave their presentations in Spanish. I was not fluent in Spanish, but wherever I sat during the sessions, the person next to me translated into English for me without any request on my part. My heart was touched over and over by these warm and loving people. It was another orchestrated event that greatly enriched my life, and I, in turn, was able to provide needed services for the caucus meetings.

During this time I was still working at the women's shelter thirty hours a week and seeing a few clients for counseling, massage, and healing work in my home. I had created a lovely and comfortable room in the basement level of our house. The large room had wood paneling, a nice carpet, comfortable chairs, and my massage table. It was private and felt nurturing to my clients and to me.

Then a surprising thing happened. As I was giving a massage to a client, the person spontaneously opened up to a memory of a past life. I intuitively stopped the massage process and began to facilitate the memory for the person. I felt strongly guided to assist her to capture the significance of that memory and the purpose for which it was being revealed. The same thing happened to other clients during that month. I intuitively knew that I was not to study hypnosis but rather to continue working with the spiritual guidance that was always available to me. Thus, I added past life memory work to my practice. I didn't plan this. It just evolved, and later I had many clients who came for a session specifically for that purpose.

During this same period I began doing healing work with my friend, Ardis, who was also a Reiki healer. Eventually Ardis and I worked together with individuals we knew or who were referred to us. Powerful experiences occurred when we worked together. We made a good team, as we had different talents which complemented each other. Sometimes we were asked to come to someone's home to heal or "clear" the energy that felt disruptive to the people who lived there. We became "ghost busters," and it was often an astounding process. Each time we followed our spiritual guidance.

In August 1980 Ardis asked me to join her in a driving trip she needed to make to New York State and Pennsylvania. I was able to take the time off from the shelter, and it was a remarkable trip. Among many other things, we spent two days at a spiritual center in Ephrata where each of us had two sessions with a psychic surgeon from the Philippines.

Probably the most impactful aspect of that trip for me was that in the space of two days three different people, each in a different city, asked me what I did. I had never met any of them previously, and when I told them I worked at the shelter for battered women, each told me they thought it was time for me to leave—that I had something else to do. I was astonished! I knew it was significant that I was being given three messages on the same theme in a short time. It was clearly guidance from the other realms.

So when I returned from that trip and went back to work at the shelter, I gave notice of my resignation, to be effective one month later on October 1. The staff was quite shocked. As for me, after four and one-half years I had many mixed feelings—excitement about my new endeavors and sadness at leaving my old friends and the program in which I had been so deeply involved. But it was time. I was tired of dealing with crises so constantly, and it felt right.

This was indeed a leap of faith because my income from my clients and occasional workshops was fairly minimal at that time. Grant and Sharon were still at home, and I needed to support them, too. Even though I felt some fear about that, I did trust that it was the right thing for me to do, so I opened myself to the adventure that lay ahead.

Chapter 4
Eight Years of Intense Spiritual Growth

During the next eight years I experienced enormous spiritual growth. It involved my memories of past lives and the facilitating of this experience for others, my study of the Kofutu spiritual healing system, expansion of my healing work, teaching and counseling, working with my Native American mentor, and the incredible process of transformation I experienced with my friend, Barb.

It was also a special family time. When I moved with my two youngest children, Grant and Sharon, to our new home in St. Paul in 1978, after the Castle Community ended, I was then fifty years old and they were respectively eighteen and fourteen. My oldest daughter, Susan, had graduated from the University of Minnesota with a fine arts degree and had moved to New York City where she was practicing her two great loves—dance and art. She was a member of the Gus Solomon's Dance Company in Manhattan, and I had the joy of being in New York for one of their dance concerts. Susan's performance was sensational.

At that time Grant was preparing to start his studies at a local community college while living at home. He was 6 feet 6 inches tall and an excellent basketball player. Two years later he transferred to Macalester College in St. Paul with a scholarship and moved into the dorm. He later graduated from Macalester, which is the college both his father and I attended. (Vice President Walter Mondale and Kofi Annan also graduated from Macalester.) What a privilege for all of us to have the opportunity to study in this outstanding college.

I learned an important lesson from Grant while he was still living at home. Our house was big and old, and I needed help with many of the chores related to the upkeep, such as shoveling, changing the storm and screen windows, mowing the lawn, doing various repairs, and redecorating. Whenever I asked for help with something, Grant would promptly say, "Yes, I'll do that now," or "Yes, I'll do that but not right now," designating whether it would be tomorrow or some time later, or he would say, "No, I won't ever do that, and don't ask me to do it again." It was fantastic! I always knew where I stood with him, which then gave me the freedom to ask him anything. I don't know where he learned that, but it provided a comfort for me, and a valuable skill that I have tried to incorporate into my life.

Sharon was then attending the open school in St. Paul and showed enormous talent in creative arts, as well as being a fine athlete, especially in swimming. In addition, she had the ability to be a creative problem solver. Eventually she transferred to our local high school and graduated near the top of her class. Sharon was also interested in Reiki energy healing and took the course from Ethel Lombardi, my former teacher.

The growth I personally experienced in those eight years in the Midwest was phenomenal. Looking back on it, I can see how orchestrated each of these experiences was.

As I have written in the prior chapter, my past life memories began to surface while we were still living in the Castle community during the mid-seventies. I will mention just a few that had great impact on my life. Probably the most important memory of a prior lifetime was having been a male Aztec Indian. This memory was facilitated by my friend, Ardis. I saw myself with bronze-colored skin. I was strong, wellbuilt, probably in my mid-twenties, and considered to be the best hunter in the tribe. I vividly remembered being out in the jungle alone, hunting. A large cat (I felt that it was a jaguar, but I did not actually see it) crept up behind me and clamped down his enormous jaws on the lower end of my spine. It paralyzed me, and I could not move. The jaguar left and did not hurt me any further. I was quite arrogant about my abilities as a hunter and my importance to the tribe, and I assumed someone would come searching for me and rescue me. No one came. I was truly helpless. I could not move, but because I was so healthy I lived quite a long time before I finally died. I cried long and hard as I relived this memory. It had been such a painful experience.

Processing this experience with Ardis, I remembered all the times in my current lifetime in which my lower back went into painful spasm that prevented me from moving very much. These spasms would typically last about five days, and then suddenly be gone. This happened about twice a year for several years. While I was living in the Castle Community, there were always people who lovingly took care of me and provided for my needs, but I never trusted it. Each time a spasm occurred I immediately became panicked, assuming I would be alone and helpless. I never trusted that I would be cared for, even though I was always taken care of. I recall one episode that was so serious I had to be hospitalized in traction for several days, but still I was cared for. Each time after the spasm lifted I would be critical of myself for not trusting that I would be cared for.

After processing that past life memory about twenty-five years ago, the spasms stopped. I have never had any further spasms in my lower back. I have been told by doctors that there is some scar tissue between the fourth and fifth vertebrae, but my back functions just fine. My deep knowing is that the purpose of my creating those spasms was to bring me back to that prior lifetime memory so that I could release and heal the trauma I had experienced. It was unfinished business for me, and now it is completed.

In many prior lifetimes I have been either or both a healer and a spiritual teacher. In many cases I have been intentionally put to death by the power structure of the time. This has occurred both when I was a peasant, and also when I held a highly respected position in my society. I have remembered being hanged, decapitated, and burned at the stake, usually when I was a woman. It was interesting to me to find that many of my clients who had health conditions related to their throats or necks would often remember a lifetime in which they had been hanged or decapitated. Considerable healing usually followed those memories.

Another issue that would come up for people in past life sessions was one of fear about making decisions. I'm reminded of one bright and talented young man who came to see me. He was from a wealthy and supportive family, had graduate degrees, and some very promising options available to him. But he was afraid to make a choice and couldn't understand the reason. He spontaneously went into a memory of having been a native tribal chief on another continent a long time ago. I had an image of him in his tribal headdress, sitting in front of me. He was immensely intelligent and beloved by his people. But there was trouble. Their large tribe was threatened by another powerful tribe, and he was faced with making a decision about what to do. Their tribe was peaceloving; their adversaries were fierce warriors. He anguished over how to protect his tribe and finally made a choice that his tribe should flee from the area. The other tribe ambushed them, killing all of his people, including him. He died feeling enormous guilt and sorrow. In this lifetime he carried over a fear of making an important decision. He wept as he processed that memory, and afterwards he said he felt like a huge burden had been lifted from him.

When I worked with clients, I always asked them what they wanted from the session. Then I said a prayer, and I called upon their spiritual guides, my guides, and invited all the angels and high beings of Light that were available to work with us, asking for the highest good to unfold for this person and that his or her desire be granted if it was in harmony with their life path. I asked for guidance to facilitate the experience, and then I followed my intuition and the awareness that unfolded. I was totally aware that I was not doing the healings. All of the healing energy comes from the Source, and I was acting as an instrument, a conduit for the energy. I believe that my spirit guides and angels directed the flow for the purpose intended.

During those years when I was facilitating past life memories for my clients, I was asked by some of my friends and clients to start a support group. I agreed, and we began to hold group sessions once a month. Before long the participants asked me to have more frequent group sessions, so we held the group every two weeks. It was not unusual for one of the members to access a past life memory during the group session.

On occasion in the group sessions, individuals told me that sometimes I took on the physical characteristics of some other person. They said I looked Native American, or Chinese, or Egyptian. Sometimes I was aware of it, but not always. I would usually catch on after awhile because of the expressions on the faces of those present.

One of the most personal and emotional past life memories I have recalled occurred on the second evening during a weekend women's retreat that Ardis and I facilitated. After our evening meal Ardis and I were talking informally when I spontaneously began to remember a life in which I had been a priest and teacher in a European seminary hundreds of years ago. My most beloved student was the priest that later became known as Saint Francis of Assisi. Francis and I had a deep bond, and the memory that unfolded for me occurred when I was in prison for heresy. I was imprisoned because I had criticized some of the church's doctrines, and I was an old man at that time. Francis was also in prison, but in a different prison from the one in which I had been placed. I had a deep knowing that Francis was dying and that he was alone. I felt such enormous grief that he was alone and I could not be with him. Deep sobs came from within me as the memory unfolded. Several years later I attended a spiritual channeling session in the Seattle area in which the man who was channeling allowed the spirit being who had been Saint Francis to come through him. Francis acknowledged me with a big smile and told me he was so happy to see me again. He validated that lifetime for both of us. The man who channeled the message did not know me and had no knowledge of my association with Francis in that lifetime.

During this period I was asked to facilitate experiences for women who had come to an intensive nine-day workshop for women that was held at a retreat center near Minneapolis. It was facilitated by two gifted women therapists who were friends of mine. I arrived on the evening prior to the seventh day, so that I could settle in and get acquainted with the group. My recollection is that there were approximately fifteen to twenty participants. I stayed overnight, and we began the first session the next morning after breakfast. The participants were ready at that point for some in-depth work. I had some experiences planned for them, but many spontaneous things unfolded, including a healing session on one of the women. It was an amazing day for all of us.

A year or two later I was again invited by the same two therapist friends to facilitate a day-long session at another nine-day women's intensive workshop. Once again I arrived the night before the seventh day and stayed overnight. We began our first session the next morning. It was a hot day in midsummer, and thus we were barefoot and wearing light summer clothing. In mid-morning we took a short break, and when we reassembled, we all sat in a circle on the lovely wood floor of this large conference room.

We began with a brief meditation. Their eyes were closed, and they followed my direction. I, in turn, followed my strong intuitive knowing, and I was somewhat surprised that I felt guided to ask the participants to focus on the back side of their hearts. I had not done this previously. In the past I had focused on the front side of the heart center. I suggested that they expand the energy out about two feet behind the back of their heart center. After a minute or two, I asked them to blend this energy with the person on either side of them, thus creating a blanket of love energy all around the back side of our circle.

Shortly after that blanket of energy was established, I heard a loud crashing sound behind me. Shattered pieces of glass were flying in every direction, and several pieces of glass landed in the middle of our circle. I quickly looked around and saw one of the women participants whom I had met the night before standing outside the glass entrance door. She had kicked the door with her boot, and broken glass had scattered everywhere. I stood up, left the circle and walked carefully over the broken glass to meet her at the door. Then I put my arm around her waist and guided her into the center of our circle. She willingly came with me, and I cleared a space for us to sit down in the center. Everyone was stunned by the shattering of glass, and some of the women in the circle were frightened and crying. I asked those in the group who were able to comfort these women to please do so, and then I asked all of them to send love to the woman sitting next to me who had broken the door. The entire group became silent as we focused healing energy to this disturbed woman.

After a few minutes the two workshop coordinators stood and led this woman out of the circle and into an adjoining private room. (Later I learned from the two coordinators that this woman had some problems, but that she had been doing very well through the earlier days of the workshop. They had called the woman's family members immediately, and the family came and took her with them for safety and treatment.) All the rest of us in the circle then processed our feelings until everyone felt calm and centered again. Except for a couple of the women who had minor little scratches, no one else in the circle had been cut or hurt by any of the sharp pieces of glass that had flown throughout the room. At that point we heard the bell ringing that signaled it was time for lunch to be served in another building. We had to walk very carefully to get our shoes, stepping over many pieces of glass. I went with several others to the dining hall, while a couple of the women stayed in our meeting room to sweep up the glass.

After lunch the women who had stayed to sweep up the glass pieces came to talk with me. They told me that after we had all left the room and they started sweeping up, they noticed that there was a precise circle where we had been sitting that was totally clear of glass shards, except in the very center of the circle. They were amazed. It seemed obvious to everyone that the love energy that each woman had projected two feet out behind the back side of their hearts, and then joined the energy of the woman on both sides of them, had created a protective shield around our circle. Since I did not ask them to create the same shield in the front of our bodies, the pieces of glass had been able to enter the center of our circle. If we had not done that, many of the women closest to the door could have been seriously cut on their backs, arms, and heads by the flying glass. As we began our afternoon session after lunch, there was a spirited discussion about the energy shield that we all had created. No one doubted the reality and power of energy at that point! I believe it was a profound experience for everyone. I was grateful for the guidance I had received and that I had followed my intuition. It was one of the most impactful group experiences I have ever facilitated.

In the early 1980s I felt the strong need to have a place outside the city, a retreat in nature. Two dear friends invited me to put a mobile home on their little farm in western Wisconsin. It was just an hour-and-a half drive from my house, and there was a lovely small river that flowed through the farm property. I had spent many wonderful times on that farm during our Castle Community years, so I happily accepted their invitation. I bought a used mobile home and had it moved to the farm.

The mobile home was in good condition. It had two bedrooms, a lovely sunny living room, but no water or sewer hook-up. I bought a portable toilet for the house and used the out house on the farm. I carried my water in plastic gallon jugs from the farmhouse, and I took showers in their bathroom. Since I had an electrical hookup and a propane furnace, I was very comfortable. I truly enjoyed the simple living and being close to nature. My collie dog and I spent many wonderful times in the quietness of that retreat place over several years, being nourished by the trees, vegetable garden, river, animals, birds, and solitude. A little later I also held a week-long summer retreat there for several women.

I vividly remember the sixth day of that retreat. Before we began our morning session in the living room of the mobile home, I noticed dark clouds gathering in the west. I suggested to the women that they close the windows in their tents, in case we had some rain. We began the session with a meditation, after which I announced that our subject for that morning was "death." At that precise moment, we heard the sound of hail on the roof. It immediately became a major hail storm, and in no time, turned the ground white with a few inches of hail. We watched the storm in silence through the windows, and I felt anguish as I saw the hail demolish the vegetable garden and flowers, which I loved so much. The storm front moved on, the sun came out, and we all went outside to walk barefoot in the hail and to commune with nature. When we came back in, still in silence, I passed out artist sketch pads, crayons and colored pencils, and asked the participants to draw a picture of death. It was a profound experience for many. Some remembered losing loved ones in this lifetime. One remembered a painful death experience in a past life. A great deal of grief work was accomplished that day. A few weeks later I had the joy of witnessing the garden renew itself. Some of the corncobs looked a bit funny, and the lettuce didn't come back, but the other vegetables continued their growth. This was a great lesson in renewal for me.

Soon after I started to spend time at my retreat home I began to receive channeled messages. I knew about channeling and had read some of Ruth Montgomery's books and the Seth channeled materials written by

Jane Roberts, but it surprised me when I began to have these experiences. My first recollection was being contacted by a being who called himself "Horace." He appeared to me in my mind and told me he was my guide. I saw him as a rather chubby man, dressed in a brown robe with a sash around his waist, and he was smiling. He definitely looked like a monk. His presence felt very loving to me, and I deeply trusted that he was from the Light.

Shortly after the appearance of Horace, I had dinner one evening with Ardis and her friend, Eve Olson. I had met Eve prior to that dinner, as she was a minister and spiritual channel at Sunday services in St. Paul. I had great respect for her, so I was delighted when Ardis invited me to join her and Eve for dinner.

At the restaurant, before the waiter came to take our orders, Eve turned to me and said, rather impudently, "You don't know who your guide is, do you?" I responded back, also impudently, "Yes, I do. His name is Horace." She laughed and told me that Horace was one of the workers, but at that moment Archangel Raphael was standing beside me and had just placed the Star of David on my forehead. The Star of David is a six-pointed star—sacred geometry. I could feel his presence, but at that time I did not know anything about the Star of David or its significance, and I did not know very much about archangels. It would be more than twenty years before I would have a profound experience with the archangels and learn that they were my spiritual family.

Not long after that evening with Eve and Ardis I began to receive messages from my spiritual guides quite often, which I would write down in a notebook. Several beautiful souls came forth at different times, and I learned the particular signal they gave me to alert me to their presence. It was a distinct feeling of pressure on each of my temples, along with a deep sense of their loving presence. Ardis and others I have spoken with have had different signals when their spirit guides are present. This reinforces for me the knowledge that we are each unique, and there are different ways that our guides contact us. A variety of Spirit Beings came to me, and I will share some of their messages throughout this book. Each time I became aware of the presence of a spiritual guide, if they did not tell me who they were, I asked for their identity and if they came from the Light. I also tuned in to the "feel" of their presence on an intuitive level. Occasionally over the years, the presence would not identify itself, or I had the uneasy feeling that the message they imparted was not accurate or from a loving source. When that occurred, I promptly terminated the connection and called on my personal spiritual guides to assist me.

The angels referred to themselves as the "Heavenly Host of Angels." The most consistent and primary presence that came to me was identified as "Sananda." I later learned that Sananda is a radiant Being, who embodied in part on our planet as Jesus of Nazareth. The following is a portion of a message that Sananda gave me in December 1980:

These times are difficult and provide tests for all who are on a spiritual path. Never has there been a time in earth's history so rich in opportunities to enhance one's spiritual growth. All children of Light must seek to bring light to every person they encounter who is open to that light. It must never be imposed, however. Offer it in love and allow each soul to choose. But do not hesitate to offer your gifts, even at the risk of ridicule and scorn.

In this transition period each soul now in physical form on planet earth will experience much sorrow at times. It cannot be bypassed. Allow the feelings to cleanse as they occur. Always remember that you are never alone. Many loving spirits are tenderly watching over you at all times.

The cosmos is ripening and planet earth is in rapid preparation for entering the realm of full planethood. All suffering will cease and love will reign. In all your decisions, remember that this is the paramount factor existing at this time. It must influence your every act.

Continue to love with an open heart, accepting the pain that comes with rejection. The ultimate goal of all souls on your planet is to increase their capacity to love without restrictions. This does not mean to compromise with one's values. Never! Never abandon your resistance to injustice, but always do it with love. You must continue in your work and will receive much guidance. Much more is available to you than you imagine. Ask for it and it will be given.

And now, rejoice with us in Spirit! Amidst all the suffering, it is a joyous time! Many souls are opening and receptive to the love that emanates from our creator. A transformation is taking place and is cause for much joy! Know always that you are surrounded with love. Continue also to love yourself as the God person you are. Peace be unto you, dear soul.

After I received that message, I was in awe. I also knew that I had not made it up because some of the language was very different from the way I would normally speak. For instance, I would never have thought to say, "The cosmos is ripening." At another time I received this message from Sananda:

The issues of power and its use are the crux of learning which must take place on this planet. When personal power needs are surrendered to the Higher Forces, the power available is increased ten-fold or 100-fold, depending on one's capacity to love. How unfortunate that so many do not see this and strive in a selfish way to gain personal power. They only limit themselves and bring unhappiness and dissatisfaction unto themselves. Love is the most powerful of all. It is so simple.

The following is an excerpt from a message I received in 1981 from Mother Mary during the weeklong women's retreat:

All is unfolding with harmony, even though there is much sadness and turmoil. We on this side are rejoicing, for the age of flowering upon your planet is nearly at hand. The time is short, and each person must act quickly to release all their limitations that prevent them from loving freely and without judgment.

You are never alone, and many loving spirits are tenderly caring for you at all times. Allow this knowing to sustain you as you struggle with difficult decisions. The tasks become greater as the time grows shorter, and each person must keep their focus upon the reason for their being on the planet at this time. Do not allow anyone to prevent you from carrying out your destiny. Listen to your guidance and trust the knowing that rises from deep within you.

The next few lines are excerpts from a message I received from Isaiah during a profound individual session that was facilitated for me by a remarkable healer in Seattle during the early 1980's:

Others will assist you in the Work, for we are never alone in our tasks. . . . This is part of a network, a much broader network than you have conceptualized in the past, for it is not just a network on your planet, although that exists and will continue to unfold, but a network that extends to infinity. . . . Many other Beings besides my essence are working with you, some of them from far distant places, and many of them who are regularly working closely in toward your planet. It is as a team with many resources from many places.

The messages I have just shared are but a few of many loving communications that have been given to me over the years. Without exception, the messages I have received have been honoring of me and all others, and they impart guidance and encouragement for all of us. They consistently have told me that we are never alone and that we are lovingly cared for. I think the challenge for us is to trust this when we are going through difficult situations. It is through challenges that we grow and develop, and ultimately our task is to grow in our capacity to love without judgments.

During the years between 1976 and 1983 I attended many workshops and conferences, including three summer annual meetings of the Association for Humanistic Psychology (AHP). I came to know many of the outstanding leaders in our country who were working with humanistic concepts focused on value-oriented human development, both on an individual basis and in groups. There was no one specific version, but my understanding is that it originally grew out of the well-known self-actualizing concepts developed by the psychologist Abraham Maslow. It was an incredible growth process for me to attend these workshops. One of the first spiritual books I remember reading was *Be Here Now* by Ram Dass. I attended three of his workshops and loved all of them. I also attended workshops fascilitated by Jean Houston, Barbara Marx Hubbard, Michael Harner, Alberto Villoldo, Virginia Satir, and numerous others. All of those experiences seemed to open a door for me to a much deeper (or higher) level of understanding.

A particularly impactful experience for me occurred during a long weekend Sufi workshop, which was led by a Sufi master. We chanted, drummed, danced, meditated, and at the end we whirled like the dervishes. Our leader prepared us intensively for two days so that we were ready to whirl. We learned how to go into and come out of the whirling without being dizzy and falling. He also wrote down when each of us stopped whirling, so that we would know how long we whirled. I went into a beautiful altered state in which I had no concept of time or awareness of the others. Many of the participants stopped earlier than I did, but I was not the last to stop. I felt as though I had whirled for about five minutes, and I was dumbfounded when I looked at the clock and heard from the leader I had whirled for an hour. Afterwards I felt peaceful, calm, and centered in my heart. I loved the drumming, and I bought a beautiful drum following that workshop, which I took to my retreat place and played often.

In 1981 Ardis and I went to Madison, Wisconsin, to participate in one of the highly acclaimed five-day workshops given by Dr. Elisabeth Kubler-Ross, author of *On Death and Dying* who was well known for her pioneering work. Elisabeth and I had a strong connection from the beginning, and her workshop impacted me greatly. I met with her on several occasions after that. One time, at her invitation, I spent a couple of days at her center in Virginia. I remember so well her playful nature as she showed me around her home; then she invited me to sit on a stool in her kitchen and talk while she was cooking. She had just returned from a trip

Jean and Elisabeth

to Europe, and she shared some of the new ideas and aspirations she had for her new center in Virginia. She especially wanted to create a place for children who were terminally ill. Her enthusiasm was inspiring. On another occasion, at a small dinner party in Seattle, I was guided to do some healing work on Elisabeth, which turned out to be powerful. The healing served the purpose of assisting her to carry out her work. To know this extraordinary woman and to participate with the other outstanding leaders I met at various conferences greatly broadened my knowledge of human behavior, helped me to develop my own spiritual concepts, and built my confidence in working with clients. I'm grateful for those opportunities.

After I woke up to my own spiritual nature and left the Universalist Church, I began to search for a new church or spiritual organization to attend, and perhaps to join. There were many options in the Twin City area, but after attending several of them I realized it didn't feel right to affiliate with any one group or one path. On special occasions I would join friends to participate in a particular event, but it was not my path to identify with any one particular organization.

In 1981 I learned through friends about a new spiritual healing system called Kofutu. It was being taught by Frank Homan, who lived in a suburb of Minneapolis. I had not met Frank, but I felt very drawn to Kofutu and so I took the next available course. This healing energy is activated by meditating on ancient symbols. When I saw the symbols and began to work with them, I just smiled. I knew these symbols; I had worked with them before at some other time and place. I was just remembering them. Kofutu is a system of spiritual growth and development which has the added benefit of healing. (There is more information about Kofutu and Reiki at the end of this book in the section on resources.)

Frank and I became good friends, and I took his classes in absent healing as well as the "hands on" touch healing of Kofutu. I greatly honor and respect Frank, for he was the channel that brought this system to the planet, which was an arduous process. As I went through the six levels of absent healing, and later the master training process, my gratitude and admiration for him became, and still is enormous.

Not long after I learned the Kofutu touch healing process, Frank authorized me to begin teaching it to friends. They were very enthusiastic about working with the symbols and energy and seeing the results. Many encouraged me to start holding classes. So I began to circulate flyers for Kofutu classes in my home. A little later Frank certified me to teach the first six levels of absent healing as well. Eventually I was asked to teach in many other cities. Different friends who had experienced my workshops and individual healing sessions in Minneapolis and St. Paul invited me to come to their city to conduct workshops and to do individual work with clients. It was a natural next step to also include Kofutu classes in these other cities. Some of these included Kansas City, Indianapolis, Dallas, and Seattle. I also held an occasional class in Philadelphia, Anchorage, on Maui, and in Toronto. I had some marvelous adventures on these trips. One very exciting experience occurred in Alaska when I was in a small plane with a bush pilot. He flew us over glaciers and as close and as high up on Mount McKinley as he dared to fly. At one point we saw an avalanche occurring below us. All of it was awesome.

Since I was eventually teaching six levels of Kofutu, I began to travel to each city at three-to-four-month intervals. I would take the level one students to level two, level two to level three, and so on. It was fascinating and rewarding for me to see the growth that occurred in my students during these intervals, and many of my students became good friends. There was always a new level one group as well. I traveled frequently, and in each city I felt as though I was visiting "family." It was a wonderful and enriching period in my life to expand my spiritual work, as well as to come to know so many beautiful people and to participate in their growth. It also became evident to me that when I traveled to these other cities my students and I were also grounding the Kofutu energy. I learned later from my spiritual guides, which Frank validated, that this was part of my assignment in this lifetime. It also became clear that Frank and I had worked together in previous lifetimes, and I had made that commitment.

One December I had the intuitive knowing that Frank, who is an enormously gifted channel, was to channel for us on New Year's Eve. I called him and asked if he and his wife had plans for New Years Eve and, if not, would he be willing to channel that evening. He accepted, saying they had no plans, and invited me and another couple to join them for the evening. It was a remarkable happening. Frank channeled three different, extraordinary cosmic souls; one of them invited us to ask personal questions. Among other topics that came up, the three others asked the guides what was their place of origin. The answer for each was a specific place, the Pleiades, for example. When I asked the question, I was told that I did not come from a place. I had come from a dimension. At that time I knew nothing about dimensions, so I asked if the guide could tell me more about that. "That information is not available to me, but the knowing is within you," the guide said. "When the time is right, you will access this knowing."

I also asked a couple of other questions. I asked about my sister, Marian's suicide, which had taken place when she was forty-two years old. I had always felt peaceful about her choice, even though it had been traumatic for me. The answer was that Marian had accomplished as much as she could in her lifetime, and another opportunity had become available for her on another continent. She chose to take it. I had learned from other spiritual teachers and writings that suicide was not an acceptable way to deal with problems. The teachings were that if a person chose suicide to end his or her life, that person would need to come back in another embodiment to deal with the same kind of problem until it was resolved. But as I mentioned earlier, I had always felt peaceful about Marian's suicide, even though it was painful for me. I was comforted to hear the guide's explanation.

I also asked to learn the reason I had chosen my parents. I had known for a long time that we each choose our parents and they, in turn, agree to bring us in and provide us with a body. I wanted to know why I did not choose a loving and peaceful home, instead of the abusive environment I experienced. The answer I was given was that in order to carry out my assignment in this embodiment I needed to develop my inner strength from the beginning. If I had been born into a loving, peaceful family, that might not have happened. I was also told that in order to carry out my work I needed to experience, firsthand, a number of the traumas that so many other humans encounter. Then, they added that I chose my parents for my genetic heritage.

Speaking of my family, during this time period in 1982, a very close friend and spiritual worker decided she would not proceed with a major plan we had formulated together. I was stunned when she announced this in a group, but I just accepted it and said very little. Other friends who were present at the time confronted me later. They told me I should have been angry. They said they no longer trusted my work in individual spiritual sessions with others, because I was not in touch with my anger, and two of them said they no longer would refer their clients to me. They also said they thought I had unfinished business with my mother (who had died nearly twenty years before that) and that I needed to get into therapy.

I felt blasted, but I also recognized there was probably truth in what they said to me. I was determined to choose a therapist who was as committed as I to her spiritual path, but all the ones I knew of were friends of mine and thus couldn't be my therapist. I had no idea how I would pay for therapy sessions either. After checking out all the possibilities I could think of, I felt totally blocked. When I admitted this to these friends who had confronted me, they replied that they thought I was just stalling and not committed to doing my own work. One of them, in a very irritated tone of voice, suggested that I look into a therapy group at the Family Renewal Center designed for victims of sexual abuse. I had not heard about this center or their program.

The next morning I called for information and went to the Center to register for the group. It was an expensive therapy program, but I filled out the application. When I went to the desk to turn in my completed application, this kind woman informed me that there were some Hill-Burton funds available for people who qualified because of low income and told me what the annual income cut-off was. I thought I might qualify, and when I returned home to check out my income for the past year, I discovered I was forty dollars under the cut-off amount. I did in fact qualify. This was definitely orchestrated by my spiritual guides.

I began participating in a weekly therapy program in a group of no more than eight women, all of whom had sexual abuse in their backgrounds. The group process was based on the Alcoholics Anonymous format, but alcohol was not the determining factor. Some of the women were fairly new to the group, and some had been working in the group for nearly a year. New members came in when there was an opening. It was an extraordinary experience for me, albeit a very painful one.

The program format required that we each write our autobiography in which we described the abuse we had experienced. At every group session each of us read an episode to the group. I remembered that it was never safe for me to be angry around my mother, for that would cause more abuse. Every week for six months I cried over yet another hurtful experience that I remembered with my mother. At one point I recall saying to one of the group members who had been in the group for a year, that I thought I would never be finished or stop crying. "Yes, you will!" she said. Interestingly enough, the greatest pain I had to release and heal was with my mother. It was physical, mental, and emotional abuse, not sexual. At least six months went by before I was ready to deal with my father's sexual abuse, which began in my early teens. There were only three episodes, which I processed and healed far more easily than the abuse from my mother.

The two therapist facilitators were excellent, but the greatest assistance often came from the other group participants. Because of our own abuse, we could spot denial and blocking very quickly, and their insight was often the most helpful. I continued in that group for fourteen months. Well into my therapy I remember one of the therapists giving me the assignment to "do my anger wrong for a month." I did not really know how to express my anger, let alone how to do it wrong. But she gave me permission to allow anger to come up and be expressed without concern about whether I did it "right." This was important in my healing process.

Toward the end of fourteen months of therapy, I also attended a couple of workshops at the Center. My children, Grant and Sharon went with me to one of those workshops, in which we looked at some of our family dynamics that resulted from my early childhood abuse. I think this was helpful to them, and it certainly was for me. I had to forgive myself for the ways in which I had been critical of my children as I was raising them. I had always loved my children very much, and it was always my intent to be a loving mother, but I had to acknowledge to myself that I made many mistakes and did some hurtful things. I did not have a good model for a mother and, even though I pledged to myself that I would never be a mother like my mother had been, some of the critical traits carried over. Years later I deeply apologized to my children, not only for the unkind things I said and did, but also for the things I did not do that would have been beneficial, and I asked for their forgiveness. (This was their choice, of course.) I have very few regrets about my life, but my failings as a mother are at the top of my list. For this I've had to forgive myself most.

I'm enormously grateful for that therapy group experience, and I know it was all divinely orchestrated. It was essential that I re-live, clear and heal those wounds. However, it was difficult to go through that process because I had long ago forgiven both my mother and father. I was fearful that I might lose my forgiveness of them, but this did not happen. Forgiveness is crucial to our healing, and I learned that I could allow all the old hurts and wounds to come up and still forgive those who caused the wounding. This was a major revelation to me.

Quite some time after I completed the therapy group process, I began waking up in the middle of the night in absolute terror. There was nothing going on in my life at that time that would cause me to be fearful, so I was extremely confused about it. As I recall, this terror continued for three or four nights before I realized there was something urgent for me to work on. I called a local friend of mine who had been trained and certified by Anne Wilson-Schaef. Anne is an extraordinarily gifted and well-known counselor/trainer whom I had met and worked with when she came to St. Paul to train the new staff at the Women's Advocates shelter in the mid-1970s. I asked my friend when she was having her next workshop and learned it would not be for several months. Well, I could not wait that long, but she told me that Anne was coming to Minnesota in about two weeks to lead a nine-day intensive workshop at a retreat center north of Minneapolis.

I thought it was unlikely that I could get in at that late date, but I called the registrar and was told that there had just been a cancellation, which opened a slot for me. I told her I would take it and then learned the cost was $550. I had no idea how I would pay for that, but later that day I received a phone call from a friend of mine named Barb. I told her the situation, and she said she would pay it for me. I was absolutely astonished, as this was a lot of money in the early 1980s. I told her I couldn't accept it because I didn't know how I would pay it back. "I didn't say this was a loan," she said. "You do not have to pay it back." I still resisted, but Barb said, "You're supposed to go, aren't you?" I knew that was true, so I accepted her offer. I called the registrar back to confirm my reservation.

The terror episodes in the middle of the night continued, and I left for the workshop with both fear and excitement. I anticipated that I would get in touch with the root of this fear promptly because of these nightly episodes and because of all the therapy I had already experienced. It didn't happen that way.

Not until the seventh day did I spontaneously go into a primal fear in which I was still an infant. I believe I was about a year old and my mother was trying to kill me, probably by suffocation. I went into blackness and knew I was dying. My young spirit also knew that I had a mission in this lifetime and that I had to have a physical body to carry it out. I was terrified in that blackness, knowing that I was losing my body. During that session I remember curling up in a fetal position and, as the therapist held me in her arms, I whimpered in a most unbelievable manner. Then suddenly the blackness lifted, I began to breathe normally again, and I knew that I would continue living. My feeling is that probably my mother got frightened and lifted the object that was smothering me. Then I went into the deepest sobbing I can ever remember. The therapist and other participants held me and comforted me for what felt like a very long time until the sobbing finally subsided and I felt released.

Shortly after I finished the experience I was taken into a lovely quiet room and given a beautiful massage. I felt exhausted but wonderful. That night I slept deeply and peacefully for the first time in weeks. After breakfast the next morning I assumed I would have an easy day. After all, I had accomplished the purpose for which I had come to the workshop.

Not so. The group had barely assembled when I began to feel very irritated by every person and everything that was said. By the time the introductory part of the session concluded, I was really angry. As we broke up for our personal work, I found the therapist who had worked with me the previous day and demanded that she work with me again. She looked startled by my demand and told me she had already committed herself to work with another participant. She said she would find another therapist to work with me, but I was adamant and already so furious that she found another therapist to help the other person.

By that time I was in a rage. She asked me if I wanted to pound on some big pillows. "No!" I yelled. "What I want to do is push you across this bloody room!" Believe me, this was not a normal feeling or response for me. I told her not to let me hurt her or hurt myself. So the therapist got two other women to support her, one on either side of her, and they all held big pillows in front of themselves. I yelled at her to resist me. The three of them stood in a line, and I lunged at them and pushed them back just a little. The therapist was taller, bigger, and much younger than I was, but I pushed her. I remember stopping in between each thrust to regroup, and each time I lunged at her, I yelled, "I will not be violated!" Little by little, I shoved her across the room.

Looking back at that scene, I'm amazed at the strength and stamina I had, and also at the rage, which I did not try to block. Actually, I probably could not have. At one point I remember thinking, "I am not in control, but I am not out of control." Even in my rage, I was aware that I was not out of control. It ended when I had indeed pushed her across the room. At that point I collapsed on a pile of pillows and sobbed for a long time. I sobbed for my little child self who had been violated by my mother. Several others comforted me, and when I finally stopped crying, I felt such release and relief. My gratitude to that therapist and the other women is enormous. I am so grateful, not just for the opportunity to clear those abuse patterns but also for the terror episodes that pushed me to work on this clearing.

Later I wondered why I had not gotten to that release while I was in the therapy group for those fourteen months. I do not know for sure, but I suspect that it may have been because I was not yet verbal when the suffocating incident occurred. As for my mother, I suspect her actions were a result of learning she was pregnant with my sister, who was born when I was twenty months old. I believe that my mother was not prepared to be my mother when I was born, and I suspect she was overwhelmed when she realized she was pregnant again.

Nearly twenty years after that session at the therapy workshop, I had an experience with my mother when she came through a gifted intuitive psychic. She apologized for all the abuse she caused me. I felt great love from her and for her, and I'm grateful to her now for the ways she prepared me for my assignment in this lifetime.

It was during this general time period that I met David and Tuieta who lived in Indiana, north of Indianapolis. Some of my friends and Kofutu students in Indianapolis told me I needed to meet this couple. Tuieta is an exceptionally gifted channel, bringing forth invaluable spiritual guidance and direction from various guides, Sananda, ascended masters, and many advanced souls. One weekend while I was in Indianapolis, a friend drove me to their home for an evening in which Tuieta channeled for a group experience. Thus began a wonderful friendship and working relationship with these truly beautiful people.

I subsequently spent several weekends in their home over the next few years, and at times we were involved jointly in some profound energy work. Many times Tuieta channeled personal information for me and others. I greatly honor Tuieta, for the invaluable guidance and information she has allowed to come through her, and David, for holding the energy for her in these channeling sessions and preparing the transcripts for publication. Later, in 1988, David, Tuieta, and I would move to Sedona, Arizona, to work on a project together, along with several others.

Another extraordinary unfolding for me was to meet a lovely

young Native American woman named Kathy, with whom I felt a strong connection. She invited me to accompany her and her two children to a reservation in northern Wisconsin for a weekend of traditional sweat lodge ceremonies. This was in exchange for one of my Kofutu classes, because she did not have the money to pay for the class. Even though I told her it was not necessary for her to pay, she wanted to exchange something of value with me. I was very excited to have this opportunity. Her tribe is Ojibwe. On the first night of that weekend I was the only non-native person present but, because I had been invited by one of their "family," all of them accepted and welcomed me to their ceremony.

Sweat lodge ceremonies are for the purification of our bodies, minds, and spirits. The sweat lodge was a simple, small dome-shaped structure that was covered with tarps and blankets. In the middle of the lodge there was a pit. Outside the lodge a large wood fire burned, and hot rocks from the fire were brought in and placed in the pit at the beginning of the ceremony. We sat in a circle on the earth around the pit in complete darkness. There were no windows, and the entrance was closed with tarps when everyone was inside. I could feel the steam curl all around us each time water was poured on the hot rocks by the leader. It was intensely hot and we began to sweat. We sang and chanted. As the ceremony progressed, we went around the circle for prayers. Each person included me, along with the others, in their prayers to Grandfather/Great Spirit. I was so touched by their acceptance and inclusion of me for the weekend. On the second night of that weekend, my beloved friend, Pat Pedersen, who lives in Wisconsin, just a little south of the reservation, drove up and joined us in the sweat lodge. It was one of the most impactful experiences of my life.

Some time later, during one of my early trips to Indianapolis, there was a powerful Native American woman present at my introductory talk about Kofutu. After the evening talk and discussion, she came to me and said she wanted to learn the Kofutu healing system but did not have the money for the class. I told her that if she felt she was supposed to be in the class she should just come, and I warmly welcomed her.

Her name is Mary Thunderwoman. I remember her telling me that she was a Native person and that there must be an exchange. It was their tradition. What she offered was to teach me some of her tribal traditions in exchange for studying Kofutu with me. She was what she called a "road person" at that time, meaning a teacher who travels around the country teaching the native traditions and holding sacred ceremonies. I was thrilled by her offer, and in a sense we became each other's mentor for awhile. She taught me so many things, and I sat with her in innumerable sacred ceremonies. The pipe ceremony was a part of her Lakota Sioux heritage. At one pipe ceremony, she gave me my Indian name: Cloud Weaver. Everyone called her Thunder.

Eventually Thunder invited me to participate with a few others on a vision quest in Texas. It was on the winter solstice, and it was an absolutely unforgettable experience. It was a cold night in Texas, even for a native Minnesotan, but fortunately I had a warm sleeping bag and an air mattress. Even though I was still fairly cold, I stayed out all night and the next day. It was the night of the new moon, as well as the solstice, and there was not a cloud in the sky.

In the tradition of the vision quest, we began with a sweat lodge ceremony in order to purify ourselves before we began our separate vigils. I had no idea where the others were taken, but after the sweat lodge ceremony I was driven by Thunder and her two apprentices in the dark to a spot in the wilderness where I was left alone. They helped me set up my space in the traditional way, and then they left.

I remember lying on my back on the earth most of the night, watching the various constellations travel across this exquisite sky while I waited for my "vision." The stars and the sky were awesome. I never received a vision, but some time shortly before dawn, perhaps around five or six o'clock, I heard a booming voice that I thought could be heard for a mile. Later I became aware that it was a voice only I heard in my head. The message was seven words:

The greatest among you are the servants.

That statement is indelibly imprinted in my memory. I stayed in my sacred place until the next afternoon and then I made my way back, returning to the group encampment. We were required to be in silence until after our briefing with Thunder and having had another sweat lodge ceremony. After that there was a feast and celebration. Beautiful sharing occurred among us, as then we could talk about our experiences if we chose to.

That vision quest was powerful for me, although there are no words to describe it. I felt that I had plumbed some major new depths in myself. A friend in Texas, who had a retreat place that was secluded, invited me to stay with her for a couple of days following my vision quest. She and her husband allowed me to be alone much of the time and just process that experience before I flew back to Minnesota on Christmas Eve.

A few months later Thunder invited me to attend a weekend Indian gathering in Indiana, at which Wallace Black Elk was the honored elder. I sat with Black Elk in two sweat lodge ceremonies—an enormous privilege, and another profound experience.

On another occasion, Thunder, who was a Sundancer, invited me to go with her and others to the annual Sun Dance at Mount Hood in Oregon to support her in the dance. The dance is a five-day ceremony, and there were hundreds of native people from many tribes and many states. I have never seen so many teepees. My friend, Pat, also came with native friends from Wisconsin. She and I sat with others in an arbor, which surrounds the circle where the dancers dance. We sang at times with the drums. Thunder invited me to come and support her again the next year at the Sun Dance. And I did. I am enormously grateful to Thunderwoman for her generous sharing with me over those years, and for her friendship.

Wallace Black Elk

During that eight-year period when I had so many wonderful and important new experiences with healing work, past life memories, teaching and counseling, I became interested in hospice work. After taking the course, I was certified to work in the hospice unit at a large hospital in Minneapolis. I clearly remember my first day in the hospice unit. The head nurse suggested that I go to each of the patient rooms and offer to fill the water carafes for the patients as a way of getting acquainted with them.

One of the elderly women asked me very directly, "Do you think it's a good idea to drink a lot of water when you're dying?" I replied that if she felt thirsty for water I thought it was just fine to drink it. I became aware that she was testing me to see what my comfort level was in talking about death. She then told me her family was out in the waiting room, holding on to her, unable to let her go. She was ready to leave and pass over, and she wondered if I could talk with them. I told her I would be happy to talk with them and asked her what she wanted her family to hear. A few minutes later I went to the waiting room and talked with her family. It was a beautiful scene, with some tears, but I could feel a shift in their acceptance. I think I helped them to accept her passing and begin their grieving process. The next week when I came in to work I learned that the woman had passed over the day following my talk with her family.

Probably the period of spiritual preparation that is most difficult to express in words are the years I worked with my beloved friend, Barb, in Minneapolis. I have such enormous honor and gratitude for Barb. Her commitment and willingness to follow her guidance and be available for the work of the Light is awesome. She and I were brought together, a connection clearly orchestrated by our spiritual guides, to go through major physical changes in our bodies in order to handle the higher frequencies of energy that were to be focused through us.

I would drive to her quiet second-floor duplex apartment in Minneapolis because it was more private than my home in St. Paul. We would spend an entire evening—I believe it was twice a week—from perhaps 7:30

until about 1:00 in the morning.

Barb had a sofa and a love seat that faced each other, with a coffee table in between. We would usually lie down, one on the sofa and the other on the love seat, while our spiritual guides worked on us. We could not see them, of course, but I could distinctly feel in my body the exact place that was being worked upon. The primary focal point in our bodies to be worked on was the neurological system, especially on the back of our necks where the head joins the spinal column. The guides also worked extensively on our hearts, because there is an electrical component in the heart. There were other portions of our bodies involved, but I can't remember them at this time. After these sessions there were many times it was a major challenge for me to walk to my car and drive home, because I felt like I was in an altered state. This process continued for at least a year.

My guides explained that my neurological system had to be expanded in order to handle the higher frequencies of energy being focused through me. They gave me the analogy of the electrical wiring in a house. You have to install different wiring in order to plug in an electrical dryer or range. Ordinary outlets of 110 volts could not handle those, and you would blow the circuit if you plugged in one of them. So the wiring has to be upgraded to 220 volts. Industrial buildings have higher capacities than that, of course, with 440 volts on up. This explanation was very helpful to me. So, my body has been rewired, so to speak, in order to act as a transformer, and that process has continued from time to time ever since. During this process, I remembered when I was thirty and had a deep x-ray treatment to my pituitary gland in order to stimulate my hormones when I was trying to get pregnant. I had the awareness that this treatment, so many years ago, had in fact assisted me in becoming prepared for the work I was to do later in my life.

During the process of these changes, I gained a little more than twenty pounds. I greatly protested this to my guidance team, but they told me I needed the extra weight for insulation of my nerve endings as I worked with these high frequency energies. They also said that when I did not need the insulation, the weight would come off the same way it went on. I was quite distressed about the weight gain and having to buy new clothes to fit me. But it was part of the process. My weight has remained fairly stabilized at the heavier level over these ensuing years, so apparently I still need the insulation. This does not happen to everyone, but it was necessary in my case. My guides gave me this message:

Allow the feelings to be experienced and released. Allow the discomforts in your body as your form goes through these massive changes. Allow the periods of confusion to be, for as yet you are unable to see and grasp the enormity of the bigger picture.

I was given extensive guidance about my diet, and asked to eliminate alcohol, red meat, coffee, and sugar from my diet, too. They told me not to drink any tap water. This meant I was not to order tea, juice, or soup at a restaurant. So I bought a larger handbag and kept a plastic quart bottle of well water with me at all times, a gallon jug of water in my car, and brought a thermos of tea with me when I went out to eat.

This was the beginning of a massive cleansing process of my body which continued for about two years. Fortunately, there was an outdoor area at a large brewery in St. Paul where there were spigots for local residents to fill their water bottles with pure artesian well water. Years later I was also guided to let go of dairy products, fish, and poultry for a few months, after which I was able to bring them back into my diet. Each time I took the step when I was ready, and thus found that it was not very difficult because it was my choice. Gradually I began to eat a small amount of sugar, and in the past two years (I am now in my mid-seventies) I added some red meat, and on rare occasions, a very small glass of wine in a social situation. I still do not drink coffee, and I have never used drugs of any kind. I am actually very healthy as a result of this regimen.

Although this long and extensive process was required for me to become capable of allowing higher frequency energies to be focused through me, I was not aware then that these high frequency energies would be directed primarily for the benefit of the Earth Mother rather than for individual people or groups. This was a new level of work for me. Many situations followed in which my energy work was directed for the earth.

A primary example of this earth energy work occurred in January

1985. I was going to Honolulu for the wedding of a very special friend from the Castle Community, and Sananda had firmly directed me to go to Maui for energy work. The day before the wedding, several of us spent the day driving around the island of Oahu. We stopped for a while at Sunset Beach to enjoy the ocean and the sun. Two others and I (one of them being a child) left the group and walked down the beach together. That beach is well known for very high waves, but that day the waves were not unusually high. However, the direction that the three of us walked did not allow us to see the waves approaching.

Suddenly we were all swept up by a "sneaker" wave, and I felt myself being lifted up high by the most powerful force I had ever experienced. I don't know how high the wave was, but it carried me way up on the beach and dropped me on the sand, face down, and then washed over me as it went back out to the ocean. The undertow dragged me—feet first and face down—toward the ocean. I had no idea how close I was to the water and if I was being washed out to sea. I felt great awe and fright at the same time.

After the wave had retreated, I looked around. I was especially anxious about the well-being of the little boy. I saw him and his mother down the beach and they were shaking off the sand from their bodies and laughing. I was relieved they were all right. I tried to get up, but I discovered my left knee had been injured. I saw two young men nearby, who had also been caught by the wave, and one of them looked right at me. I called to him and asked him to assist me. He ran over and helped me get up, and assisted me to limp to higher ground on the beach. My friend saw what happened, and she quickly came to help me. I placed my hands on my knee and did healing work all the way back to Honolulu in the car. It was a painful injury, but I was able to go to the wedding.

Three days later I flew alone to the island of Maui in order to go to the top of Mount Haleakala for energy work. I stayed in a hotel, which was not far from the airport, and one night my guidance directed me to drive to the mountain. While I was alone in the observation building on the top of the mountain at about 5:00 a.m. in the dark, I felt myself merge with the mountain and become one with her. My role was to allow the high frequency energies to pass through me in order to open up the energy flow in

Jean in crater of Mount Haleakala

the mountain. I learned later from my spiritual guides that the energy flow in the mountain had been intentionally shut off long ago by beings of the Light because the energy was being misused.

It was very cold up there that night, and even though I had worn some warm clothing, I got chilled. Within a few hours after the energy work was completed, I came down with major cold symptoms and totally lost my voice. I could only speak in a whisper for about a week. My guidance told me later that in merging with the mountain I had taken on her silence to facilitate the transition for Mount Haleakala. The whole experience was quite profound.

When I left Maui a couple of days later, I flew to Seattle for about ten days to teach classes in Kofutu and to work with individual clients. That week in Seattle was a major challenge for me because I had to teach in a whisper. Fortunately, all of my students were able to hear and to understand me.

Arrangements had been made about a month before I flew to Hawaii for me to go north to Orcas Island in the San Juans after my teaching and client schedule in Seattle. A couple of nights before I left for Orcas Island, my spiritual guides came in and told me that while I was on Orcas I needed to go to the top of Mount Constitution. They said that I was carrying energies from Mount Haleakala which needed to be connected with Mt. Constitution. My friend, Joan, accompanied me. My Orcas Kofutu class was on Saturday, and the next day my two Orcas friends drove Joan and me to Mt. Constitution. I had never been to Orcas before, and I was enchanted with the island. As we began driving up the mountain, we saw a light snow covering the mountain. Part way up we came to a lovely lake—and a large gate. The road was closed to drivers wishing to go to the top of the mountain. I felt shocked and concerned about my ability to carry out my assignment.

My island friends told me there was a powerful and beautiful energy spot at the other end of the lake, and they suggested that perhaps the energy work could be accomplished there. My knee was still somewhat disabled, but since it was level ground, I felt I could walk to that energy spot. We knew there was no way we could walk to the top of the mountain. So we began walking on the path along the shore of the lake. The other three could walk faster than I could and were ahead of me when I felt a strong physical "tugging" on the upper back of my coat. I was startled because I knew there were no other people in the area.

Turning around, I found myself standing alone, but my attention immediately went to a beautiful, big, ancient cedar tree. I walked back to the tree and asked the tree if it had "called" me. It said, "Yes." (I don't know yet how that tugging on my coat was accomplished.) Then I heard clearly in my head, "Have no concern about not getting to the top of the mountain. The work will be accomplished anyway." The tree had communicated this message. I was very relieved and thanked the tree profusely as I hugged it. Then I set off down the path to join my friends, who at that point had come back to find me. I gave them the message from the tree, and we all rejoiced.

When we arrived at the special energy spot, we stood in a circle, held hands, and prayed. I opened myself to the energy process, and as the energy was released I heard in my head, "Thar she blows!" I nearly exploded with laughter, because I had just come from Maui where I had seen whales for the first time. I was ecstatic seeing so many humpback whales, both adults and babies. When the energy connection was completed, we ate a picnic lunch, and then walked back to our car at the other end of the lake. It was a fantastic experience. Shortly thereafter, Joan and I left the island and drove back to Seattle. The next day I flew home to Minnesota.

About six weeks later I flew to Indianapolis to teach Kofutu classes and see clients. While I was there, I drove north to see Tuieta and David. Tuieta channeled information from her guidance team that the sneaker wave had been an attempt by the forces not aligned with the Light to prevent me from getting to Mount Haleakala for the energy work. I had had that feeling, but still I was comforted to have it validated.

After the long and intense period of changes I experienced with Barb, my spiritual guides asked me to sell my house and move to Seattle. This was in 1984. I was completely open to this request for several reasons. First, my house had become a burden to me. Grant had graduated from Macalester and was now married to Raenay. They had their own home. Sharon had graduated from high school and had moved to Mankato, Minnesota, to attend that branch of the University of Minnesota. During her freshman year she applied for and was accepted into a program in which she would spend her entire sophomore year living in northern England. Her classmates and students from other U of M branches all lived in an old Castle for that year. It was an accelerated program, and the students were given many two-week break periods which enabled them to travel around Europe. Following her sophomore year, Sharon spent the summer traveling alone in Europe. It was an experience filled with adventures for her.

So at that point in my life, I did not need to provide a home for my children. Besides that, I was often traveling around the country, teaching Kofutu. And each time I left I had to make arrangements for someone to care for my dog, house, and yard. It was a big house. While I did have a few house-mates during those years who could help, I was ready to move on. I have always had an adventurous streak in me. I had lots of good friends in Seattle, and I loved the mountains and being close to the ocean. But mostly, I wanted to follow my spiritual guidance. So it was an easy choice to sell my house and move to Seattle, even though none of my family had ever moved away from the Twin Cities. I promptly listed my house with a realtor. Over the next fourteen months I had two potential sales, but both of them fell through. Finally the sale was accomplished in June 1985. It was not quite time yet to move to Seattle, so I moved temporarily to my little retreat place in rural Wisconsin. During the following few months I continued traveling to various cities to teach and hold private sessions with clients. In between those trips I enjoyed the quietness, the closeness to nature, and the communion with my friends in the other dimensions.

On one of my trips to Seattle, I told my friends there that I had been guided to move to Seattle and that it would probably happen in the spring. They were very happy I was coming. Some of them advised me that when I moved to Washington State I would need to have some legal protection in order to do hands-on healing. This was not required in Minnesota at that time. My choices were to become ordained as a minister, become a licensed massage therapist in Washington State, or a licensed counselor. I chose to be ordained as a minister. My dear friend, Joan, recommended I see a remarkable woman named Dorothy Sinclair, an ordained minister, who had been guided about twenty years earlier to start a non-profit spiritual organization. The new board named it the New Age Fellowship. Dorothy and her husband owned a piece of property in Seattle. On it was their home, and next door was a chapel where they held classes, church services, and weddings.

Joan took me to meet Dorothy in order to talk about my ordination. I liked her immensely and was very impressed with the organization's process of ordaining new ministers. I remember Dorothy telling me that part of their mission was to ordain applicants who were already doing their spiritual work so that they would have legal credentials without going through several years of traditional seminary training, which was not in harmony with their spiritual beliefs. Each applicant was asked to write a letter to the board of five members, discussing two subjects. The first set of questions asked: What have you done with your life, what are your credentials, and why do you think you are qualified to be ordained as a minister? The second questions asked: What is your purpose in wanting to be ordained? What can't you do now that you would be enabled to do if you were ordained?

When I got back home, after pondering these questions for a long time, I wrote a four page, single-spaced letter to the board of the New Age Fellowship. The procedure was that each of the five board members would read the letter. At their next monthly meeting, each would share their response to the applicant's letter. Then they all would go into meditation and ask for guidance as to whether or not it was appropriate for the Fellowship to ordain this person. Ultimately, that is how they made their decision. I was accepted for ordination and became ordained shortly after I moved to Seattle.

During those years of intense physical changes and earth energy work, my spiritual guidance consistently told me several things. First, they said my needs would always be provided for, and that has proven to be true. There have, however, been many times when I was right down to the wire and my faith got tested in a major way. They also said that they would never interfere with my ability to honor my commitments. Also true. Two other phrases they frequently used were:

Be gentle with yourself.
Just allow.

They told me that all of us who have made a commitment to serve the Light are tested on many levels. We are tested for our faith and commitment; our purity of intent and motive; our capacity to love; and our endurance. Perhaps there are more, but these are the ones I remember. Our performance in those areas is what determines the level of assignments we are given. They have often told me that I am a way-shower and a front-runner.

A consistent theme in the spiritual guidance I have received is that our goal is to expand our capacity to love without judgment. This requires that we let go of fear, for fear has a paralyzing effect that prevents us from being centered in our hearts.

It also requires that we release negative terms. My guides have consistently referred to the forces who are not working with the Light as "Forces not aligned with the Light." They have never called them "evil" or "dark," or any other negative term. In one message from Sananda, he said the following:

Hear me, for I come in great love for ALL ONES, for my love has no limits, no restrictions, no judgments. I urge you to be mindful at all times that this is your task—to release your limitations and judgments—in order to allow the Universal Love to flow through you—for ALL ONES, for all are my beloved and precious ones and there are no favorites. None are more special, nor more favored. All are one in Creation, and all are beloved. As one rises in their consciousness and awareness of who they are, this truth becomes more evident.

Another important piece of guidance was how important it is that we both give and receive. There must be a flow. My tendency is to want to give, but in the past I was not a good receiver. When I got my lessons about having to receive, I discovered that I felt much more powerful when I was giving, and I felt humbled when I was on the receiving end. That was a revelation to me.

As I write this, I remember receiving this information during a session with a client:

*The deepest knowing is beyond thought;
therefore, it cannot be translated into language.*

This helped me to understand why it was so difficult sometimes for me, and others, to put into words the things we know at some deep level. It is because that "knowing" is not in the realm of thought.

Finally, in the spring of 1986 it was time to move to Seattle. My friend, Joan, was going through a transition in her life and asked me if I would like to share a house with her. I was delighted. She began looking at houses to rent, but she could not find a suitable one prior to my leaving Wisconsin.

Meanwhile, two wonderful friends, Judith and Myrna, offered to drive with me to Seattle. Myrna rode in my car, and Judith drove her car, which pulled a low trailer that was designed to be a canoe carrier. We piled all of the things I needed to take with me into these vehicles, and the rest I left behind. When I sold my house the prior year, I gave away almost all of my furniture and accessories.

Because I had trips planned during that six-week period prior to the closing of the sale of my house, there was no time to organize a garage sale. So I invited my children first and told them to take anything they wanted. Next came my good friends, and so on. I trusted that I could replace whatever I needed in my new home. It was amazing to me how many of these pieces were offered to me later in the same way that I had offered my things to others. It was a beautiful lesson, which demonstrated that what we give to others comes back to us.

I cried when I said good-bye to my children and beloved friends, but I also felt an enormous excitement about my new adventure. Even though I encountered many challenges and scary stretches, I have never for a moment regretted my decision to leave the Midwest and begin this new chapter in my life.

Chapter 5
Seattle and Sedona

My trip from Wisconsin to Seattle in May, 1986 was wonderful and filled with surprises. We took the northern route through North Dakota and Montana. As Judith, Myrna, and I were approaching the area just before the turnoff to Yellowstone Park, I received a message from Sananda asking us to detour south and go to the park. We stopped, got out of our cars, and talked about it. Then Sananda gave more information about the reason for the detour. He said that enormous pressure had built up in the earth in that area, and if the pressure was not released, there would be massive destruction and devastation. He directed us to go to the Old Faithful geyser, so that when the geyser erupted, energies would be focused through the three of us that would assist the pressure in the earth to be released.

We all agreed this was very important and wanted to follow this guidance. We turned off the freeway and headed for the park. Just before we entered the park area, we reserved a motel room. Judith left her car at the motel, and we three piled into my car. We quickly hit the road and drove toward Old Faithful. Myrna had been there previously and knew the park, but it was the first visit for Judith and me. During the drive through the park I felt major stress in my body, as Spirit was preparing me for this transmission of energy. After we arrived and parked the car, we literally ran to the place each of us felt guided to go. We were spread out in three places around the geyser; I couldn't see either of my companions. The park had just barely opened for the season, so there were few visitors. I remember seeing only three or four in the area to which I felt intuitively guided.

Then the geyser erupted. In a loud voice I was spontaneously saying, "Release, Mother," over and over, with great fervor. I felt the release, and I felt a deep connection with Mother Earth. After the geyser finished erupting, I realized how tired I felt and found a park bench to sit on and rest. It wasn't very long before the three of us found each other, and shared our experiences. We went into the big lodge for a short time, and then drove back to our motel. By then it was dark. We were tired and hungry, so we had dinner at a restaurant before we went to bed.

The next morning we went to a place that had a hot spring. We soaked and played in the water for quite awhile. It was great. Then we headed back to the freeway that would take us to Seattle. I called Joan and learned that she still had been unable to find a suitable house for the two of us to rent. Myrna, Judith, and I had friends we could each stay with in Seattle, so we would be well provided for in any case.

Not long after our arrival Joan bought a Seattle paper on a day when there were many real estate ads. She made calls, and we looked at a couple of houses. There was one in particular that sounded perfect for us. It was the first ad the landlord had run, and he invited us to come and see it. We knew that house was the one for us. However, many others had come to see it too, so we had to wait for his decision. He and his wife invited us to come back again, interviewed us extensively, and then rented the house to us. They owned and lived in the house right next door, and both properties were on the shore of Echo Lake in North Seattle. The house was empty, so we were able to move in immediately. Since Joan had ample furniture and household items, I didn't unpack very many of my things. There was a large garage in which I stored my boxes and stuff. We were so grateful for that lovely house on a beautiful little lake, and we knew it was divinely orchestrated for us to get it.

Joan is an artist, so in the third bedroom near the front door, she set up her studio. I put my desk in there as well. She had a portable screen that I could use to create a private place in the living room where I could work with my clients. We loved being close to the lake. It was such a small lake that there were no motorized boats allowed on it, so it was quiet. A few people had kayaks and canoes. The lake was deep and the water was clear—perfect for swimming. We had our own dock. During the summer, I swam across the lake almost every afternoon after my last client session. I loved it. What a beautiful introduction to living in Seattle.

Very shortly after we moved in, some time near the middle of May, our guidance told us it was urgent that we go quickly to Mount Baker to the north of Seattle. They told us the mountain could erupt any time, which could have been very dangerous since the World's Fair, Expo '86, was being held in Vancouver at that time. We were not even fully unpacked when we took off with Joan's camping gear to camp for the weekend on one side of the mountain. It was beautiful. We were asked to do the same thing the next weekend on a different side of the mountain. We went to still another side of the mountain on the third weekend. I feel quite sure that many other people were also guided to go to the mountain for the same purpose: to help stabilize it.

Our friend, Jennifer, offered to fly Joan and me, along with our friends, Ron and Steve, in a small airplane to the remaining south side of the mountain. Ron and Steve owned a metaphysical crystal shop in Seattle and brought many small crystals with them. It was a beautiful clear evening, and Jennifer flew as close and as high up on the mountain as she safely could. We all dropped crystals out the window onto the mountain. Mission accomplished. And, as of this writing, the mountain has not erupted.

On June 23 I was ordained as a minister by Dorothy Sinclair, along with three others, in a beautiful ceremony in the chapel of the New Age Fellowship. A few years later the New Age Fellowship merged with an international spiritual organization called The Council of Light. After the merger the joint organization was called The Council of Light.

A few days later Joan conducted one of her Nature Spirits workshops. Mark, who was a Kofutu student and dear friend, and I were the only participants, which was most unusual as she typically had quite a number at her workshops. She took us to a beautiful park area near Puget Sound. As we were connecting with the nature spirits by a group of trees, I suddenly felt myself being called. I looked behind me and knew immediately that this large, stately tree was calling me. I left Joan and Mark and went over to the tree. The trunk of the tree was partly down an embankment, and there was a tall chain link fence between the path where I stood and the tree trunk. I couldn't touch the trunk of the tree, but some of its large branches barely touched the top of the fence.

The tree said to me, "Thank you for the work you are doing." I had never felt so acknowledged before in my life. Then the tree melded its energy field with mine. We merged in a state of oneness. It was the most profound feeling I had ever had. And then the tree took me to the next step. I merged with everything in the universe—in all of creation. I don't know how long I was in that state of oneness. I felt ecstatic in a way I never had before. I was no longer separate from anything or anyone. I stood there, clinging to the fence, with tears streaming down my face.

I had learned many years before through my spiritual teachers and readings that everything in all of creation is one. We are not separate from anyone or anything. But I had now experienced it at the core level of my being. I bless that tree for facilitating the most sacred experience in my life to this date. My life was forever changed.

Then I began to be aware of Joan and Mark standing on either side of me by the fence. They could feel the energy and saw my tears. With great difficulty, I found my voice and shared with them what I had just experienced. Later, when Joan and I got home, I felt disoriented and very emotional. Since then I have read several accounts written by people who have had a near-death experience and gone to the Light. They experienced the bliss of being "Home." Then when they were told they had to come back to their earthly bodies, each one said they didn't want to leave and felt devastated to be back in their bodies. That's how I felt—devastated. I wondered how I could function again on the earth plane after having this experience.

Joan was very kind and nurturing, but I felt that no human being could help me at that moment. In desperation, I called out to my spiritual guides and angels for help. When I asked, "What am I to do now?" Sananda came in with this message: "Go facilitate this for others." I had no idea how I was to do this, but within the next six weeks Joan and I created (with our spiritual guidance) a weekend retreat called "An Experience in Oneness."

We began working on ideas and plans within a day or two. Always we asked for guidance, and always we received it. It was an amazing process. Someone suggested that we call a retreat center that was only about a thirty-minute drive east of downtown Seattle. We called and learned they had an opening for us on two weekends—one toward the end of August and another about a month later in September. This availability was almost unbelievable to us. We reserved both weekends. Both Joan and I had previously facilitated many workshops and retreats, so we had many rich experiences from which to draw in our planning process. Then, of course, we had to create a brochure. We worked together on the text, and Joan (the artist) designed a beautiful layout and logo. The resulting brochure was lovely.

As we were planning the program, Sananda told me that we must have a sacred pipe ceremony in the Native American tradition. He explained that the pipe was the most perfect symbol of oneness on the planet at that time. The bowl of the pipe represented the feminine and the earth; the stem represented the masculine and the connection to Source (Grandfather). I asked Joan if she knew someone that carried a sacred pipe, and Sananda quickly told me that I was to have a pipe and conduct the ceremony.

I was dumbfounded. I called a friend in Minnesota to ask if she knew where Thunderwoman was and learned she was in Texas. Thunder could have been anywhere on the road, and here was a friend who gave me the phone number to call. I called Thunder and explained what was happening. She supported me in carrying a sacred pipe and invited Joan and me to come to Mount Hood the next month to support her in the Sun Dance. She said one of her apprentices was there in Texas with her, and she could go to the shop where I had gone to get my supplies for my vision quest. She would pick out a sacred pipe for me and bring it to the Sun Dance.

Even though the way was provided so easily for me to receive the pipe, I felt unready and resistant. "If I'm going to carry a sacred pipe, I want one that was made in my homeland, Minnesota," I said to Thunder. She said she would convey that to her apprentice. When her apprentice went to the shop, she learned they had just received a new shipment of pipes that were made in Minnesota. She asked Spirit to guide her as she selected a pipe for me.

So many changes had happened in my life very quickly. I had moved to Seattle, had been ordained as a minister, had experienced my Oneness, was planning to facilitate weekend retreats with Joan, and now was preparing to go to Mount Hood for the Sun Dance and to receive a sacred pipe. Joan had not been to a Sun Dance, but she was eager to go with me. In July we drove together to Oregon. It was another profound experience for me. That pipe was dedicated at the Sun Dance. Not long after its conclusion, Thunder and her three apprentices came to our home in Seattle and stayed a few days. We planned a ceremony to consecrate the pipe I was to carry, and I called many friends to join us in our home.

It was a powerful ceremony. The sacred pipe was smoked by each of us, and its energy blended with the pipes of Thunder and her apprentices. Then Thunder wrapped up that pipe in a shawl and gave it to me, instructing me to spend time alone with it to get acquainted. A day or two later Thunder, Joan, and I went to visit a friend of Thunder's in Seattle, and there we met a man named Fred. Fred is not a Native American, but when he was a little boy his mother moved her family to the Nez Perce reservation in eastern Washington after Fred's father had died. As a young boy, Fred often sat at the knee of Little Big Man and grew up learning the Native traditions. During his adulthood he had often been a liaison between the Indians and the white establishment. He was a few years older than I and, at that time, was traveling and living in a camper truck. Fred became friends with Joan and me, and he came over to visit us from time to time in our home.

Joan and I were preparing for our retreat, and I expected to spend time with the sacred pipe. However, it did not feel right to take the pipe out of the shawl in which it was wrapped. I didn't understand this. A few days later, Joan and I spent a day on Whidbey Island, which is just north of Seattle. Joan had been guided to create a sacred staff for the retreat and needed to get something in nature with which to make the staff. I sat in a secluded spot by the water of Puget Sound, expecting to unwrap the pipe. I could not do it.

Then Sananda came in with a message. He said the pipe I was carrying had a different purpose. He told me this pipe was to be a bridge between the old traditional ways and the new paradigm which would unfold on the earth. It was to be an inter-dimensional pipe. Therefore, I was not to unwrap the pipe at that time. I was to cleanse the pipe of its old energies and to allow it to be filled with the new frequencies of energy. He said I could smoke it or not—that it was my choice. Its purpose would be served whether or not it was smoked.

I had no idea what to do next. The following morning Fred stopped by to see Joan and me. I told him I had been directed by spiritual guidance to cleanse the pipe, but I did not know how to do it. Fred told me he knew what to do, but that I should not ask him to cleanse the pipe until I knew what it was to be filled with. He said if I did not fill it immediately after the cleansing, the pipe might be filled with energies that would not be in harmony with its purpose. Sananda guided me about the new energies to fill the pipe. Very soon Joan, Fred, and I arranged for a trip to a nearby mountain, which Fred selected, to carry out this guidance. I was unable to climb as high as Fred had intended, but Fred found a beautiful and secluded spot that was perfect for the ceremony.

We set up the sacred circle. Fred then disappeared into the forest with the pipe and some other objects. Joan and I could not see him and awaited his return. He came back to the circle and handed me the pipe. I immediately stood, held the pipe up high, offered the pipe to Creator Source (Grandfather) and stated my intention and commitment for the purpose of this pipe. I called upon my spiritual guides to fill the pipe with pure energies and to assist me in carrying out the purpose for this sacred pipe.

I had felt very insecure and unready to carry a sacred pipe prior to that ceremony, but as I made my commitment and declared my intention for the pipe, I felt incredibly empowered. It was a Divine blessing I will never forget. Fred and Joan also blessed the pipe. At the conclusion of the ceremony we closed the circle and packed up all the sacred items. We ate a picnic lunch in celebration and then departed. Walking down the trail to the bottom of the mountain I felt wonderful.

Fred was walking just ahead of me, and I called out to him, "Fred, how many times have you done this?" He called back, "I have never done this before. And I have never known anyone who would even consider doing what you have just done." That stopped me in my tracks. He explained to me later that no Native person would ever break the tradition as I had just done. So much for my empowerment and confidence! But as I pondered all this and asked for guidance, it was clear that this pipe truly did have a different destiny. For whatever reason, I had been selected to be the person to break the tradition and carry an inter-dimensional pipe. I felt a huge burden, for I deeply honored the traditional ways, and I did not want to offend Thunder and others who were walking the traditional path.

In succeeding days, as I sat and communed with the pipe, I made the decision to not smoke it. I had never been a smoker, and I knew several people who wanted to come to the pipe ceremony but who, with great difficulty, had stopped smoking. They told me they felt concern about the possibility of again triggering their addiction. Instead, as I held the pipe (after the traditional cleansing with smoke from sage, cedar, sweet grass, and tobacco), I offered the pipe first to Great Spirit/Grandfather, then to Mother Earth and the four directions, and then I held the pipe with the bowl touching my heart center and the stem extending upward and touching my forehead on the "third eye." As I passed the pipe, most others who sat with me in ceremony followed this pattern. It felt honoring and very precious to me.

I broke still another tradition. In Native ceremonies women who are on their moon (menstruating) are not allowed to sit in the circle. It did not feel right for me to prohibit anyone from coming to a pipe ceremony for that reason; therefore, my ceremonies were open to all. Some time later when I spent time with Thunder in Dallas, I told her about my decision to not smoke the pipe and to welcome women to the circle who were on their moon. She was upset with me for breaking the traditions, but I felt deeply that I must honor the intuitive feelings and spiritual guidance I had received that this pipe had a different destiny. I felt that I was answering a higher calling.

In the Native American tradition, I did create my own pipe bag. I have never been a good seamstress, but Joan helped me with it, and I did much of the cutting and sewing. I chose to use white deerskin for the bag, and created a long fringe. It turned out to be quite beautiful. The following summer when I was visiting my friend, Pat, in Wisconsin, she created some beautiful beadwork for the stem of the pipe and made two small bags from the white deerskin. One bag held sage, and the other held cedar. All were decorated with colors, including lavender, soft turquoise, pink, blue, and white. These colors were different from the traditional black, yellow, and red, but the colors that Pat and I selected felt more in harmony with the purpose of this inter-dimensional pipe.

Joan and I continued preparations for our first weekend retreat. Many people had made reservations, and everything was falling into place. Besides the local people who registered, my friends, Jean from Dallas, Judith, Pat, and my daughter, Sharon, from Minnesota were coming. After they arrived in Seattle, we all gathered for a pipe ceremony on a nearby beach on Puget Sound. I felt a little awkward in my first experience holding a pipe ceremony, but it was lovely and also felt very right. Judith brought me an exquisite large eagle feather she had found on a wilderness canoe trip in Canada, which I used in my ceremonies.

Both of our retreats were wonderful experiences. We provided many and varied activities, including singing, chanting, drumming, dancing, painting, and meditating. Each evening after our program activity was completed, we asked the participants to remain in silence until breakfast the following morning.

The primary experience occurred when we asked each participant to choose a partner. In each couple one partner was blindfolded, and the other partner led the blindfolded one on a walk around the beautiful nature setting. This was done in silence. Eventually the leading partner led the other to some particular tree, one that person could then get acquainted with and commune, but could not see with their eyes. They were encouraged to allow a bonding to occur and to feel their oneness with the tree. When the blindfolded partner felt complete, the other partner guided them back to the place where the blindfolding took place. Then the blindfold was removed and the formerly blindfolded partner went looking for their tree. They always found it, and it was an awesome experience for several of them. Then the process was reversed, and the previously blindfolded partner provided the experience for their partner, who now was blindfolded. This process provided an opportunity to build trust in themselves, their partner, and their ability to establish meaningful connections with other forms of life.

In the closing hours participants shared and processed their experience.

And they took part in a pipe ceremony, followed by a joyful celebration before they departed. We received great responses from the participants, and Joan and I felt happy about our experiences and our work together.

Before Joan and I held our first retreat from August 22 to 24, we had a surprise visit from an older woman, Sister Thedra, whom I knew about from David and Tuieta. I had been eager to meet her. Sister Thedra had been guided by Sananda and other spiritual masters many years ago to move to Mount Shasta in northern California and set up a center there. She created an organization called Association for Sananda and Sanat Kumara (A.S.S.K.), through which she held classes and gatherings. She was not a nun, but Sananda had guided her to adopt that name. On that particular day Sister Thedra was in Seattle for another event and came by to see me. Thedra, a tiny little woman with a huge presence, was in her late seventies or early eighties, and she had been channeling Sananda and other masters for nearly thirty years. She had published these writings long before most other channels began to do so. She invited me to come to Mount Shasta for a gathering she was holding just a short time later.

Pat Pedersen and Jean

The gathering occurred the weekend following our first Oneness retreat. My friend, Pat, from Wisconsin, two others, and I drove down for the gathering and camped in a nearby campground. David and Tuieta came from Indiana to be present also. It was my first experience on Mount Shasta. What an awesome energy spot that is. Tuieta, David, and I were guided to leave the gathering and drive high up on the mountain for energy work. We did this a couple of times during the gathering.

During those summer months in Seattle I was not teaching Kofutu because Frank Homan had created study materials so that students could learn the system with a workbook. Thus, there was a moratorium on classes. It felt strange to have no classes, but I was busy with Joan preparing for and holding our retreats.

Joan and I were guided to make a trip together by car, taking the sacred pipe and her sacred staff with us. We left on October 1, just a week after our last retreat, and we were gone for nearly four weeks. We camped all along the way, and in the wilderness areas we did a great deal of energy work. It was a circle trip, taking us east to Montana, then south through Yellowstone Park and the Grand Tetons, east to Utah and Arizona, then west to California, and finally, back up the West Coast through the redwood forest to Seattle. We met so many fascinating people and held pipe ceremonies along the way. My daughter, Sharon, had come back to Seattle from Minneapolis to house-sit for us, caring for Joan's dog, two cats, and our plants while we were gone. While there, Sharon decided to stay in Seattle. She found a place to rent and moved in the day we got back.

After returning to Seattle, I began to see clients again for healing and past life memory work. Many of my clients had quite profound experiences. Some of them had the incredible and exquisite experience of going back and remembering their origin in the Light, their oneness with all of creation. That is truly a transforming experience. And sometimes a person would remember working on various projects in other parts of the universe or would remember doing something in a past life that we humans do not now have the capability of doing. They would thereby understand why they were feeling pulled to do particular things now—things which did not make sense to their rational mind.

I also felt the strong knowing that it was time to start doing energy transmission work in group sessions. I scheduled them once a month to be held in our home. During these sessions we would all go into meditation, and I would open myself to allow the energies to flow through me. Several of my friends and clients attended, and many of them had some pretty awesome experiences. The groups were well attended, with a fairly large core group that attended each month.

It was not long after this that Sananda came through to me and said:

Release every system, every technique or practice you have ever learned. Let them all go. Your next step is to align yourself directly with the God Source and allow yourself to be an instrument.

I was stunned and promptly asked, "But what will I put on my business card?" He was gone; I got no reply.

I got this message just when I was sending daily Kofutu long distance healings to a friend in Minnesota. I had performed two of the five healings and felt committed to completing the remaining three sessions. However, the next day, when I prepared to send the third healing, I discovered that I was completely disconnected from the energy source. I was shocked, to say the least. I could not send the healing to her. What followed was disbelief, anger, confusion, and sorrow. I felt that I had let my Minnesota friend down by not completing the series of healings I had promised her. I called her that evening, and before I had a chance to tell her what Sananda said, she exclaimed with joy, "The healings worked!" She did not know that I had not completed the series of healings, but she was happy with the results. Then I shared with her the guidance I had received from Sananda and told her I felt I had not fulfilled my commitment to her. She said it did not matter, because the purpose of her request for the healings had been accomplished.

That was a major lesson for me. My trust level became much higher from that point forward. It was a beautiful example for me that I would never be guided to perform, or not to perform, anything that would adversely affect any one else. My trust level soared, but I still did not know what to put on my business card. I had been in the process of planning a new card, and Joan said she would design it for me when I had the information prepared to display on the card. Eventually this did get completed, and the card was beautiful.

I didn't know how to explain to Frank Homan that I was disconnected from the Kofutu energy and that I needed to be released from the Kofutu master healer training process. I had been in this training process for over a year, and it was very difficult for me, to say the least. There were many times during that training period in Minnesota when I felt like everything in my life was turned upside-down. My daughter, Sharon, and others who were living in our home found me extremely difficult to live with during that time.

Fears also surfaced in me about how my Kofutu students would respond. As a matter of fact, some of them were angry when they learned I was not working with or teaching Kofutu any longer. I also had fears about whether I would have enough client sessions to support my living expenses. It was a very scary time for me and a major test of my faith in myself and my spiritual guidance.

Then my friend, Ron Lane, invited me to a dinner party in his home where I met Krysta Gibson. She had started a monthly newspaper in Seattle a couple of years prior to that time, which she called *The New Times*. I really liked that paper. It contained fascinating articles and interviews with people who were working with spiritual and holistic activities. One day Krysta called me and told me her spiritual guides had asked her to also start another newspaper called *Spiritual Women's Times*,[1] which was to be published quarterly. They guided her to carry an interview with me in the first issue, which came out in March 1987. The title Krysta chose for the interview article with me was a statement I had made, "We all have a purpose for being here." In the interview I shared some of my history and a great deal of information about what I had learned from my spiritual guidance, and from my own experiences as well as those of my clients.

I was startled to see my interview and photograph on the front page. But I was gratified by the response it received—the many calls from people who wanted to schedule a personal session with me and to attend the group energy circles. Once again my needs were provided for. Not long after that first issue was published, Krysta ran a beautiful interview article about Joan on the front page of *The New Times*. Joan also received a similar response, increased client sessions, and orders for her beautiful channeled mandala-shield artwork.

That same year my guidance asked me to make two trips back to Maui and Mount Haleakala for further energy work. A different friend went with me on each trip. It was intense but definitely more fun than the first trip I made alone. On each trip we were invited to stay in the homes of women I had met on my first trip. I loved being in Hawaii.

During the spring and early summer of 1987, a great deal of information written by Jose Arguilles was being published about the Harmonic Convergence. The Mayan Calendar predicted this powerful time on the planet for mid-August, 1987. Ron Lane and I were invited by Krysta to write articles for *The New Times* to assist others in preparation for this momentous event. I had never considered myself to be a writer, but I did have information I wanted to share with readers. Ron and I collaborated, and each of us wrote separate articles for the paper that covered different aspects. Krysta published them in two issues during the early summer months. She also invited me to write other articles, and over the next couple of years I wrote several articles that were published in *The New Times*:

> *How To Deal With The Changes*
> *Service or Servitude?*
> *The Right Use of Power*
> *An Update on The Changes*
> *Toward Being All You Can Be*
> *Preparing for The Christ-Mass*

A reprint of the article *How To Deal With The Changes* appears in the back of this book. (The suggestions I included are still relevant and may be helpful to readers who are feeling challenged on a physical, emotional, or mental level.)

Prior to the Harmonic Convergence I flew back to Minneapolis for a few days and had the joy of being with my oldest daughter, Susan, for the birth of her first child—and my first grandchild. Susan had left New York City a few years prior to that time and had moved back to Minneapolis.

I arrived on July 27, just as she was beginning her labor. I went with her to the hospital and stayed for the entire labor process. Susan was in the midwifery section of the hospital where the rooms were like hotel rooms. When she was close to giving birth, Susan lay on the double bed and I sat on the bed behind her, leaning back against the headboard. I held my daughter in my arms as she gave birth to her son. It was one of the most beautiful and joyous experiences of my life, never to be forgotten. The next few days I stayed with Grant and Raenay in their home and often went to be with Susan and her new baby. I was so happy and grateful for this wonderful time with my family.

Soon after I returned to Seattle, I talked with David and Tuieta on the phone, and they told me they had received spiritual guidance to be with Sister Thedra and others in California for the Harmonic Convergence. A wonderful couple had opened their spacious home that could accommodate quite a large group of people. Tuieta asked me if I wanted to join them. I checked in with my guidance and was given confirmation to do so. David and Tuieta met me in the Los Angeles airport. We rented a car and drove a couple hours northeast of Los Angeles to the lovely home of Ed and Dorothy. My recollection is that we arrived a day or two before the first day of Harmonic Convergence. We knew there was significant energy work to be done. Sister Thedra arrived with others the next day, having driven there from Mount Shasta.

It was quite a gathering of people, a meeting of different ages and backgrounds. We gathered on a hillside adjacent to the home for meditation in the early morning and in the evening each day we were there. We could feel the energies being focused, and it was often very stressful on my body. I rested quite frequently during the day. Everybody pitched in and helped with food preparation and cleanup. At times during the day we gathered to share stories and information, and at least once, Tuieta channeled. It was a powerful experience for us.

Shortly after I arrived back home in Seattle, Joan and I made the decision to move from our home on Echo Lake. Our landlord needed to raise the rent because of an increase in taxes, and that made it too expensive for us. Since Joan had been invited to share a home with her daughter, her partner, and some others, she chose to do that. I then sought out a new home for myself. There were some interesting options, but as a result of the incredible way it all unfolded, I found myself homeless for about a month. Of course, I really was not homeless because friends invited me to stay with them temporarily, but for the first time in my life I did not have an address, and I did indeed feel homeless. It was very humbling and somewhat frightening. As a result, I have a much deeper awareness now of what it feels like to be homeless.

One of the men who regularly attended my energy circles told me he had room at his home and invited me share it with him. His house was in a suburb east of Seattle. I appreciated Jeremy's offer and very shortly moved in. I think that was near the end of October. In addition to my bedroom, there was a small room I could use for my personal client sessions and a family room where I could hold my group energy circles and sacred pipe ceremonies. It worked very well. In December I received a phone call from Dorothy and Ed in California. They were inviting everyone who had been to their home for the Harmonic Convergence to come back there after Christmas for a follow-up gathering. I had told Jeremy all about my experience there in August, and he was very interested in also attending the gathering.

Jeremy and I drove down, and on the way we stopped for lunch in northern California. While I was eating a bowl of soup, I suddenly had an experience unlike any previous one. I was psychically contacted by a being from a different planet. These beings have physical bodies but do not have emotions. Their existence is mental. This being and others were observing humans on planet Earth with great interest. I do not remember much of the conversation now, but I reported what I was learning to Jeremy who was sitting across the table from me. I continued eating my soup. In the midst of this, the waiter came to our table, and Jeremy simply told him to bring me another bowl of soup. He knew that when I channel I usually get hungry. This experience continued for a few minutes after I finished my soup. It was very interesting, to say the least. (Some time after that experience I learned that there is much interest around the cosmos about what is happening on our planet because we humans do have emotions.) After we were back in the car, Jeremy drove, as I felt quite spacey.

David and Tuieta were not at the gathering, but many of the people from the August Harmonic Convergence were there. Sister Thedra rode down with others from her Mount Shasta center. There were some wonderful discussions and personal sharings. Thedra needed a ride home, because the friends she drove down with were not going back at that time. Jeremy and I decided to take her with us and drive to Mount Shasta.

Before we left Dorothy and Ed's home, Sister Thedra told me there was a woman named Ginny that I needed to meet. She lived in California, on our route back home. She called Ginny and arranged for all of us to meet for lunch. I sat next to Ginny in the restaurant, and at one point I turned to her and said, "Ginny, we have something to do together." She felt the guidance also, and we exchanged phone numbers.

Jeremy, Sister Thedra, and I resumed our journey north to Mount Shasta, and we ran into a rather severe snowstorm. At one point we barely missed a very big truck that swerved and ended up blocking the highway. We got around it just before the highway patrol closed off the highway. I was driving at that point, and even though I had many years of experience driving in Minnesota winters, it was challenging for me to drive in the mountains with this precious older woman sitting next to me. Thedra was relaxed because she knew we would be taken care of. It was after midnight when we arrived at Mount Shasta, so we stayed overnight at Thedra's home. The following day Jeremy and I drove on up to Seattle.

In early January I called Ginny. We made arrangements for her to come to Seattle, so we could explore what Spirit had in mind for us. Since Ginny had a great deal of experience facilitating workshops, we created a new workshop together. We held one in Seattle and another one in northern California. Ginny had a spacious motor home, in which she enjoyed traveling. So when she asked if I was interested in making a journey around the country with her in the motor home, I promptly said I would love to. I had wanted to travel in a motor home and be a gypsy for a long time. At that point Jeremy was in a new relationship with a beautiful woman, a friend of mine, and he really wanted to have his home to himself again. It was a perfect time to start a trip with Ginny, so I packed up my belongings and put most of them in a storage locker in Seattle.

We left in mid-April, stopping for several days to spend time with a mutual friend in northeastern Washington. Then we began a long journey which took us eastward through Idaho, Wyoming, South Dakota, and on to Minnesota, where I stayed with Grant and Raenay for a week while Ginny flew to Miami for a workshop. The furthest east we traveled was to visit David and Tuieta in northern Indiana, then we circled back to Los Angeles, stopping for several days in Sedona, Arizona, where we arrived on the third of June.

Everywhere we went, I was continually touched by the beauty of this country. It was such a gift to have the opportunity to be so close to nature in many places, to park overnight by streams, and to rejoice in the sunrises and sunsets over mountains, valleys, and deserts. I felt myself slowing down, getting more in touch with my natural rhythms, being very present in the moment, and more thankful than I've ever felt for the privileges and gifts I receive constantly. I had fun learning how to drive the motor home, and I was only scared when heavy winds would hit us broadside.

On our first evening in Sedona I sat outside on Sister Thedra's patio with my notebook as I went into my evening meditation. Sananda greeted me: "Welcome home, beloved sister." I replied, "No, I'm just visiting." A few months earlier, Thedra had been directed by her guidance to sell her home and center at Mount Shasta and move to Sedona. Thedra and several others from her center did move there, and I knew that David and Tuieta were also being called to move to Sedona. I resisted the idea of leaving Seattle, which I loved, to go live in Sedona. I had been to Sedona on a brief trip a year before, and I remember saying, "This is a great place to visit, but I'd never want to live here."

The day before Ginny and I left Sedona, Sister Thedra fell, injured her back, and was hospitalized for a few days. We spent time with her in the hospital before departing, but Ginny and I needed to get to Los Angeles for a major event to be held on June 11 at the Coliseum so we said goodbye. The event was called "Starlink 88." Tuieta was on the program and channeled Lord Michael. I shared an apartment with David, Tuieta, and their friend, Coletta for three days. During rehearsals, I was an instrument for setting up energy patterns in preparation for the June 11 planetary increase in vibratory level, and so I walked around the inside of the Coliseum many times.

Following that event, Ginny and I spent ten days in several places in southern California. We co-led a workshop on "Co-Empowerment" in the San Diego area. On June 21, as we were driving, I suddenly had the strong intuitive feeling that I needed to call Sister Thedra in Sedona. We pulled into the parking lot at a 7-11 where I could use the telephone. I found out from Harold (who took care of the house, did the cooking, and cared for Thedra) that he had been trying to reach me. He needed to leave for two weeks to attend a family reunion, and Sister Thedra wanted me to come and care for her while he was gone. Since Ginny and I had completed our commitments, I was free to leave. I flew to Sedona the next day. That ended my two and one-half month, 7,000 mile journey with Ginny. I will always be grateful for that glorious adventure.

Spending those weeks with Thedra, hearing her stories and learning more from her wisdom, was a precious gift. She was a truly remarkable woman, and I was inspired by her. She had been incredibly courageous in following her guidance, in spite of numerous health challenges, personal hardships, and ridicule. Caring for her was challenging for me, however, because Thedra had very decided food preferences and ideas about how things should be done.

Once again, during my first evening's meditation, Sananda began his message with, "Welcome home, beloved one." Once again, I replied that I was just there in order to care for Thedra. However, during that two-week period it became very clear to me that I was definitely to participate in the next

Sister Thedra

chapter, in Sedona, with Thedra, David, and Tuieta, and the others who had been called there. I began to feel more comfortable in Sedona and to appreciate the high desert country. Another divine orchestration, for sure.

While I was there with Thedra, Tuieta left Indiana and flew out alone to Sedona to find a house to rent for David, herself, and Coletta. She asked me if I would like to share the home with them. I was happy to do so. Tuieta and I looked at a few houses, but none of them were suitable. We saw one that felt right, but the owner was in California, and the house needed considerable repair and redecorating. When Tuieta left to fly back to Indiana we did not have a home secured.

After Harold got back to Sedona to resume caring for Thedra, I returned to Seattle. My possessions had been in storage for nearly four months while I had been on the road. My daughter, Sharon, agreed to drive down to Sedona with me in my car. One of the men in the Sedona group who needed to make a trip to Seattle would bring my belongings back with him pulling a small U-Haul trailer behind his truck.

Sharon and I left Seattle on August 8. We had a lovely trip along the Oregon coast and through the Redwoods. We visited friends in California and then drove to Sedona. We arrived in the afternoon, and David arrived that evening. He and Tuieta had sold their house in Indiana, and he had brought all their furniture and belongings with them, all of which were contained in a huge truck with a trailer attached. He also brought their dog and cat.

The next morning we put the cat and dog in a nearby kennel, and then I took David to see the house that Tuieta and I had looked at weeks ago. A truck was parked in the carport. We discovered the owner and his friend had also arrived from California the night before. They were already painting and fixing up the house. The owner agreed to give us a one-year lease, and he allowed us to unload everything in David's truck and trailer into the living room of the house after a couple of days, even though he felt they would not be finished in the house for still another day or two. Many friends from Sister Thedra's organization helped us unload, so we were all in by the twentieth. Another miracle!

David had to leave the day after we unloaded his truck to meet Tuieta in Chicago. They had several workshops scheduled through the fifteenth. We didn't know yet when Coletta would be arriving. I brought the cat and dog home from the kennel, and Sharon flew back to Seattle about three days later. I unpacked the basics and settled in for three weeks alone with the cat and dog. I was tired and needed rest, so I appreciated the quiet and solitude. Even though I was surrounded by mounds of boxes and a jumble of furniture, it was livable. Gradually I unpacked and moved furniture around to create the feeling of being home before David and Tuieta arrived. The house was a large two-story building, and my bedroom was on the upper floor. We had a panoramic view, and out one of my windows I could see Cathedral Rock. We were in a quiet area on the outskirts of town and not very far from Sister Thedra's home. Coletta joined us later.

Sedona has several major vortexes of energy, so we expected there would be high-energy work to be accomplished. That was definitely the case. It was not an easy year for any of us. There were many times when Tuieta, David, and I felt stretched absolutely to our limits, or beyond. I soon realized why I had been reluctant to move to Sedona. This was one of the most stressful and challenging periods in my adult life. I felt more vulnerable than ever before, but, paradoxically, I felt strong in my vulnerability.

David set up a new computer system in our large office on the lower level. I spent about fifteen hours a week transcribing tapes of Tuieta's channeling sessions into the computer. David then prepared them for publication. I felt very enriched in this process. This was the first time I had worked on a computer, and even though I only did simple word processing, I felt I had developed a very important skill. It was exciting to finally be doing this.

I also put in about fifteen hours a week at Sister Thedra's home to enter Thedra's channelings into her computer, which dated back to the

Jean near "Cathedral Rock"

123

1950s. Her channeled material had been typewritten over the years, and the paper was no longer in good condition. Once again I was grateful for my typing skills. Near the end of that year my spiritual guidance told me that while I was typing Tuieta's and Thedra's channeled messages I was also balancing my left and right brain in the process. They said that I tuned in with my right brain to the energy and beingness of the one who was communicating the message, and my left brain put it into a good sentence structure as I typed.

Tuieta began to hold her channeling group sessions, and we had a large circle. We came in silence and left in silence. Very powerful teachings came through Tuieta. I was grateful for the contact I had with others in the Sedona area who were seriously working on their spiritual path. Our work was so intense that it left little time or energy for me to reach out to the community. This was a very different pattern for me. But the energy work was intense and challenging for all of us. One time several of us were guided to go to the Grand Canyon for that purpose. The canyon's awesome beauty could not ease the fatigue of a long day. We were wiped out afterwards.

While I was living in Sedona, my guidance team told me that they had been experimenting to see if they could focus energies through me for other parts of the planet while I was in Sedona. It was successful, and therefore my energy work could be greatly expanded. I no longer had to travel to different places in order for the energy work to be accomplished. That year when there was another serious crisis in the Middle East, I had been plugged in for energy work in that area. Sananda gave me this message:

> *ALL is in Divine Order. Even that which does take place in that area in which I did abide, that which you know as the Holy Land, the Middle East, is unfolding according to the Father's Plan. The suffering, as brother raises his hand upon his brother, is not of the Father's Plan, but as he gave all ones choice, the drama that is now unfolding there is in Divine Order.*

In July 1989, after living in Sedona for a year, I was told by my guidance that I had fulfilled my portion of the work there and that it was my choice to continue to live in Sedona or to move. They could now work through me in whatever location I chose to live. Needless to say, I meditated on this. David and Tuieta were guided to stay for another year. I considered several options, and within a fairly short time made the decision to move back to Seattle. I had mixed feelings because I loved my friends in Sedona. But I longed for the many lakes and rivers, the ocean, the green of trees, shrubs and plants, and the snow-capped mountains—a landscape so different from the desert country of Arizona. It had not felt right to go back to Minnesota or to start out in an entirely new place. So I moved back to Seattle. Looking back on that year in Sedona, I have such enormous respect and honor for David and Tuieta. They made some courageous choices, and their commitment to their spiritual work was total. They will always be an inspiration to me.

In August I moved with my belongings back to Seattle, and I put my stuff in a storage locker. My special friends in Seattle once again opened their home to me while I looked for an apartment. Soon after I arrived I received a call from a woman named Linda, asking for a private session with me. She lived in a suburb north of Seattle. After that session in her home, she asked me if I would be interested in house-sitting for her while she went to Colorado for a week to attend a seminar. I accepted, and along with the house, I took care of her cat.

A few days after Linda left, she called from Colorado and told me her guidance indicated that she and I had some work to do together. She suggested I settle in for awhile. I checked this out with my guidance, and it was affirmative. It also felt like a good base from which to look for an apartment. When Linda returned home, we were plunged, it seemed, into an accelerated process of changes that would allow our energy vibrations to be increased. It was not the same, but it felt as intense to me as the time I spent in Sedona. And it felt a bit like an extension of the process I had experienced with Barb in Minneapolis a few years before. Fortunately, both of us were able to allow ourselves to be quiet, without demands upon our time. I was grateful for the haven of Linda's home and for her companionship as we went through the experiences of those massive changes. Even so,

I longed for some relief in the intensity of the changes, and desired a home of my own. I needed my own haven. After a month or so, Linda also needed her privacy and to resume other aspects of her life.

Searching for an apartment, I was discouraged, and it took far longer than I had anticipated. But finally I found a suitable apartment in a different suburb of Seattle, and signed the rental agreement in spite of a higher rental price than I had expected. At that moment I had no idea how I would pay for this, as I had exhausted almost all of my financial resources in Sedona. I just knew I had to have a home, and I trusted that somehow the way would be provided. There were times when I definitely was scared, however, and I had to really practice "allowing."

It was a very nice apartment in a quiet location. It provided me with a totally new experience, as I had never lived in an apartment before, or lived alone except for the brief periods I lived alone in my mobile home on the farm in Wisconsin. Since I had practically no furniture, I was grateful when a friend of Linda's, who had lots of furniture in storage, offered some of it to me for use in my apartment. It reminded me of when I passed on all my furniture and other home furnishings in St. Paul. I knew I had to manifest some income right away too. I was at a friend's home the next Sunday and looked through the Sunday paper's want ads. I didn't know where to begin but soon realized that the only kind of job for which I was qualified (that I could find right away through a want ad) was secretary.

There were nearly a dozen columns for secretarial jobs, and I thought it would take me the rest of the day just to read them all. I firmly asked my guides for help. I pointed to the top of the first column and asked, "Is it in this column?" I heard the answer, "No." I followed the same procedure with the second and third columns, with the same answer. When I got to the fourth column and asked, I received the answer, "Yes." Then I slowly ran my finger down the column and asked them to stop me when I got to the right one. Almost to my surprise, they instructed me to stop about two-thirds of the way down. I read an ad for a part-time secretary at a research center, which was located near the University of Washington. I didn't want a full-time job, and I didn't want to be downtown. That sounded perfect to me. The instructions were that applicants should apply in person at the Center.

The next morning I drove to the Center, loved the campus-like feel of the property, and noted it was not an impossible drive from my apartment. I walked into the designated office and was greeted by a pleasant young man who handed me an application. Two other applicants were there, both were far younger than my sixty-one years, and both were dressed like professional secretaries. Each woman whipped out her resume and efficiently began to fill out the applications. I didn't have a resume because I had been a self-employed counselor for many years after working at the clinic and the shelter. I had no recollection of the dates, my salary at each previous job, or my supervisor's name. I filled out what I could and then told this nice young man that I would need to look in my files for some of the information. He said, smiling, that this was no problem and that many applicants took the application home to complete it. Whew! I left his office, walked around the campus a bit, and drove home to search through my old files. I drove back the next day and turned in my application.

Not long afterwards I received a call requesting that I come in for an interview and to take some typing and secretarial tests. I was delighted and a bit nervous, even though I knew my typing skills were excellent. I also thought I had great computer skills, having transcribed all those tapes. Little did I realize what I would need to learn. I performed very well on the tests, and I enjoyed the woman who interviewed me. I liked the feeling of the Center, although it was clearly a very intellectual campus and a totally different environment from my previous twenty years. They told me they would call me later after they had tested all the applicants.

Meanwhile, I had made reservations to fly to Minnesota the first of November for a week to see my children, my new little grandson (Susan's baby), and my dear friends. I knew I could do that before starting my new job if I was hired. A couple of days before I left, I received a call from the Center and was asked to come in for an interview with the director of the particular project for which I had applied. We scheduled my interview to take place just before I drove to the airport for my flight. I was fascinated by the research the director was doing on the sociological implications of organ transplants, and he was very interested in my experience in community. Following the interview, I gave them a phone number where they could reach me in Minnesota, and I left for the airport.

While I was at Pat's home in Wisconsin I received a phone call from the Center, saying they would like to hire me. I was elated. We made arrangements for me to report for work shortly after I returned home to Seattle. I would work four five-hour days per week, totaling twenty hours. As a part-time employee, I would not receive benefits, but I figured that schedule would allow me time to see clients and to begin holding my energy groups.

I came back from Minnesota with a bad cold; I had completely lost my voice and could only whisper on my first day at the Center. I was taken to the office I would occupy, and the man in charge of all the computer training and maintenance came in first thing to tell me about my computer. He asked if I had experience working on a network. "No," I said, not having the slightest idea of what he was talking about. He said that was okay, that many excellent secretaries had never worked on a network. I realized then how limited my computer skills were. An important part of my job was to create tables and insert data from the research teams. I felt as if I was in way over my head. For a month or more I was in a high state of stress and panic. Fortunately, my co-workers were friendly and kind.

After all my years doing personal and group counseling, workshops, teaching, seminars and retreats, this secretarial job was absolutely foreign to me. But I did trust there was a purpose for my being there, besides the fact that I needed the income. Not long after I began working on the network, a web that allowed me to hook up to all the scientists, my spiritual guides informed me that high frequency energies were being focused through the network as I worked. The Center itself was also located in a strategic place for high-energy work. Once again, all was in divine order, and after a couple of months I began to turn out beautiful tables of data and felt confident with the work I was doing on the computer.

When I was not working at the research center, I frequently worked at home on a small Compac computer that was given to me at Sister Thedra's center before I left Sedona. I was unable to finish entering all of her writings into the computer before moving to Seattle, so I brought them with me. It took me a few months to complete them.

I vividly remember a time when I was working on Thedra's writings that all of a sudden I experienced the most overwhelming feeling of grief. There was nothing occurring in my life at that time for which I felt grief, so I rather impatiently attempted to stop it. Immediately I got a message from Sananda in which he told me I was not clearing my own grief. He said I would be clearing grief for untold numbers of others who were unable to do so for themselves, and he kindly asked me to allow the feelings of grief to be released through me. I let go and literally sobbed for many minutes. Then I stopped, and before long I was able to resume my work on Thedra's writings. This process has occurred quite a few times in the succeeding years, and friends have told me they have had similar experiences in which they felt they were crying for someone other than themselves.

During these months I had very few clients, because I had been gone from Seattle for a significant time period. But as soon as I resumed holding the monthly energy groups, they were well attended. I also started a weekly women's spiritual support group, which met at the home of one of the women. The five or so women and I became a strongly bonded group. We all grew enormously that year as we shared our feelings and insights about all the changes that were happening to each of us. Some of those changes were traumatic, and our mutual support was invaluable. One of the women would frequently say to us, "But the final chapter hasn't been written yet!" when any of us were anxious about the outcome of a particular situation. I have never forgotten that phrase. I have shared it with many others over the years, and they in turn remind me when I get uptight about something. That thought, that phrase, has really helped me so many times, for we can't see in the moment what benefits will unfold as a result of any particular painful or challenging situation.

In July the next year I had a major stressful episode with my heart. This was not the first time, for my heart had been greatly impacted by the energy work in the preceding two or three years. But this episode was more serious, and after a day or two of trying all the things I knew how to do, it was clear I needed some medical help. I had not had any health insurance since I left Women's Advocates about fifteen years prior to that time, so I didn't know how to proceed. I called some doctors' offices, to which friends had referred me, and was told that, as a new patient, I could not be seen right away. One kind woman suggested that I just walk into the emergency department of a big hospital in downtown Seattle. The one she suggested had a discount program for those who qualified on the basis of income.

I had not seen a medical doctor for many years because I had been working with naturopathic doctors and other healers. It was a scary decision for me to go to this hospital, and I called several friends to see if they could accompany me. Not a single one of them was available to go with me for various good reasons. With fear and trepidation I drove to the hospital alone about noon. I filled out the necessary papers in the emergency room and very shortly was taken into an examining room. To say I was nervous is an understatement. At that particular moment there were very few people needing attention, so I was given the most wonderful care by several nurses and technicians. Besides checking my vital signs and learning about my symptoms, they engaged me in friendly conversation, which helped me to relax. An extremely kind doctor came in, and after examining me he ordered some tests.

Before all of the tests were completed, there was suddenly an avalanche of patients who needed immediate attention. A nurse wheeled my gurney out into the hall to free up my room for another patient. I was feeling better, but I still needed to lie on the gurney. From that vantage point I could easily observe the activities of the nurses, technicians, and doctors as they worked with the other patients. My heart was so touched by the kindness and beautiful care I witnessed and the cooperative interactions between the various staff people. They worked as a loving team together. I was inspired. Prior to this experience in the hospital I had developed some negative attitudes about the traditional medical establishment. Because I had gone to the hospital alone and had no other support person with me, I was totally dependent upon the medical staff, both physically and emotionally. This would not have happened if a caring friend had been with me. I was very aware of the divine orchestration of this experience, and as a result I came away with a deep appreciation for the medical staff. I definitely had an attitude adjustment.

The tests determined that I was not in any danger with a heart condition, but I was asked to come back for some further tests. I agreed to this without any remaining fear. I was advised by the medical doctor to stay home and be quiet for a few days, which I did. I felt a little shaky when I returned to work at the research center, but I was okay. The various tests determined that I have a condition called atrial fibrillation. From time to time since then I have had other "episodes," as the doctors refer to them. I need to be quiet and rest for a period of time until my heart feels healed and is back in balance. These episodes seem to occur when a particularly intense period of energy work has taken place. In recent years I have learned that taking natural liquid hyssop is extremely beneficial and efficient in dissolving any clumping of the platelets that has developed in my blood.

In September of that year, 1990, a good friend in Seattle asked me if I would like to spend a three-day weekend with her on Orcas Island in mid-September to celebrate her birthday. I had not been back to Orcas since that phenomenal experience at Mount Constitution several years earlier, and I was delighted to join her. During the week prior to our departure for Orcas, another Seattle friend suggested that I contact a friend of hers named Nina, who lived on nearby San Juan Island. I had heard about San Juan Island, but I had never been there. I called Nina to ask if I took the ferry to her island could we perhaps meet over a cup of tea for a couple of hours? She said absolutely and invited me to stay overnight at her home. I was amazed, but also had a feeling this was being divinely orchestrated.

The friend who was having her birthday was perfectly happy about my being gone for one of those three days, so that is what happened. While I was in Nina's home in Friday Harbor I met several others who were friends of Nina's and part of the island's spiritual community. They invited me to come back and lead an evening workshop for this group, which I did in early October. I shared some of my spiritual experiences and guidance, and then led them in a meditation. Nina invited me to again stay in her home for the weekend and to facilitate private sessions with some of these people in her extra bedroom. Thus began my connection and work with people on San Juan Island.

I loved the island and the people I met. Its natural beauty—its beaches, small mountains, and views of both the Olympic mountains and the

Cascade mountains —captivated me. I felt a much deeper connection with San Juan Island than with Orcas Island, though I was aware of the special uniqueness of each. The friends I met through Nina soon began to feel like family. Nina invited me back a couple more times that fall, and I facilitated another evening workshop in November.

Back in Seattle, at one of our weekly women's support group meetings in December, a most unusual thing happened. We always closed our group sessions with a fairly long meditation, followed by a sharing of our individual experiences. One of the women turned to me after our meditation and said, "You're going to move to that island!" I was dumbfounded. "Oh no. I love to go there to visit, but I'm not going to move there," I said. But that is what she saw in her meditation. A few days later, when Nina and I were talking on the phone together, I told her what my friend in the group had said to me. "Well, of course, you're going to move here," Nina replied. "I've just been waiting for you to get it!" She invited me to share her home with her, and I was astonished.

Christmas was approaching. I still worked at the research center, but the project for which I had been hired would be completed soon. I was working hard at that time, but there was no indication that there would be additional work to keep me employed there. I kept thinking about the island, but I did not know what I would do to support myself financially on the island, and I truly loved the Seattle area. Obviously, the unfolding of the events that led me to the island could not be denied, and as I have said earlier, I love adventure. But what on earth would I do on that tiny little island? What was my purpose there?

I kept mulling over all these thoughts and got nowhere with a decision. I finally realized I would need to go back to the island for a weekend after the holidays to get clear about my next move. That worked for Nina, and I spent the first weekend in January at her home. I felt desperate to reach a decision, and my spiritual guidance team said nothing. I was on my own; I had to make the choice. By the end of the weekend I decided to move there, even though I felt scared about it, and as I drove back to Seattle I developed a plan of action. The following day I talked with my supervisor at the research center and gave notice that I would leave at the end of the month.

That was not a problem, and I agreed to work a few extra hours that month to complete the project. That evening I contacted my apartment manager and gave notice that I would vacate by the end of the month. Again, no problem.

It was a busy and hectic month. Several friends came and helped me pack, and I made a reservation to rent a small moving truck. I could not have made the deadline without all the help I received from friends. During that month I got a call from my Minnesota friend, Judith, saying she was coming to Seattle at the end of the month. When I told her I was moving to the island, she laughed and offered to help me move again. All sorts of people helped me load the truck and do the last cleaning. I was so grateful for all the kind assistance from my friends. However, there was no time for me to process my feelings about leaving Seattle. I just packed up and left, and it was another leap of faith on my part.

1. (pp.115) *The New Times* and *Spiritual Women's Times* are no longer in print. Krysta Gibson now publishes the *New Spirit Journal*.

Chapter 6
San Juan Island

Judith and I left early on that morning, January 31, 1991, and arrived at Nina's house before noon. Three new island friends were on hand to help us unload the truck. Afterwards we ate a lovely lunch that Nina had prepared, and then Judith and I got back on the ferry to take the truck back to the mainland. It was a long day and we were tired when we finally returned to Nina's home that night to rest.

There had been two horrendous snowstorms in the previous six weeks that caused considerable damage and power outages to Seattle as well as most of the Pacific Northwest. This is a rare occurrence in this part of the country. Parts of the island looked ravaged, with scores of trees down, and I heard many stories of hardship from various islanders. I took Judith on a tour around the island before she had to return to the mainland. Then I started the process of settling in and resting from the hectic pace of the past month. I definitely felt some fear about my move and what lay ahead for me.

Nina and I were asked by our guidance to sit down for extended meditation in the late morning every day, and we did this. I remember that we meditated together again in the evening for a shorter period. On February 8, 1991, just a few days after my arrival, Sananda gave me the following message during our meditation:

My beloved sister, whom I cherish,
Be of good cheer and be joyous in all of your endeavors and tasks. Devastation is occurring on your planet, but we rejoice in the large numbers of ones who are awakening and opening their eyes and their hearts. Sadly,

many others are becoming even more rigid in their belief that there is an evil one who is responsible for all of the turmoil and trouble. (He is speaking about Saddam Hussein and the Gulf War.) They find comfort in having someone to blame for the hardships, and this occurs in every land and in every group of people. More lessons have they to learn, and the opportunities will be available and the models of love and commitment to the Source, to the Oneness, will be there to show them the way if they choose to follow.

Blessed ones, we are preparing this tiny island for a major role in this area for the energy changes which are forthcoming. It will be a fortress, a sentinel, a haven, a pivotal launching point. More information will be given in increments in the coming days. We wish only now at this time for you to know that you are involved with us in a mighty work in the unfolding of the Father's Plan.

As you have been told, many additional ones from many realms have joined the brigade, so to speak, to augment the strength that is needed to carry out this project. It will succeed, for the Father has deemed that it be so.

My blessings and my love to you beautiful ones who keep the faith. You have great strength and much compassion. You are blessed indeed.

Now be at peace and know that you could have no priority that is more important than the work that you do with us at this appointed hour. All is well. Adonai

I did not really comprehend what Sananda was telling me about this island, but I felt such overwhelming love from him as the message came through. I had made my choice to move here, and I trusted there was clearly a purpose for me and for the island. Later, in a meditation on April 8, I received this message from the Heavenly Host of Angels, which again referred to the preparation of this island for future events:

Beloved one,
We speak with one voice—we who are your beloved friends from many realms. There are untold multitudes that work with you and others

who have chosen to be available for the preparation of this island. It is becoming a citadel, a mighty fortress that will weather the forces that will be unleashed as the Earth Mother lets go of the tensions within her. The work in this place is of a profound magnitude, and thus there have been many called to assist in its completion.

Before moving to the island, I had already scheduled a trip to Indianapolis to take place a few weeks after my move. While there, I facilitated a workshop and worked with clients. I also led a workshop in Seattle on the way. This provided me with some needed income. After I returned to the island, I had a few client sessions and worked at a couple of temporary jobs offered by new friends.

One day in May I had a profound experience with orca whales—those beautiful black and white whales. I had heard a lot about them for several months, but I had not yet seen them. I learned that the three resident pods typically arrive in late April and leave at the end of September.

That particular day I had all afternoon free, and it was a beautiful sunny day. So I took a sack lunch and headed out by myself to explore the west side of the island, which is the area where the whales are most often seen. I started out at Lime Kiln State Park, known as Whale Watch Park. It was beautiful, but I saw no whales. Then I drove to the county park. As I left the parking area and walked toward the sea, I saw a large black fin surface quite a distance out in the water. Then I noticed others. I felt such excitement to at last witness these beautiful creatures, even though they were far in the distance. They were swimming rapidly, and before long they had disappeared out of my sight.

I drove to the British Camp area next to explore and to eat my lunch. As I was leaving British Camp, intending to drive to another park, my guides told me to go back to the county park. I protested, telling them I had already been to the county park. They kept saying, "Go to the county park." So I turned and drove back. I was astonished to see at least a couple dozen whales close to the shore, and they were playing with each other. Later I learned that the whales had probably just finished feeding. There were a few other people in the park, and we all laughed with great joy as we watched the antics of the whales. I was just thrilled.

The whales began to leave, swimming south in the direction of Whale Watch Park. I watched them until they had all left the area, and then I decided I would drive south also to follow them. As I approached the water near the park, I saw three female whales playing in a small bay. It is easy to tell if an orca whale is male or female. The female has a large curved black dorsal fin on its back, and the male has a straight-up dorsal fin, which can be six feet high on a mature adult. When the whales are fully grown they can be thirty feet long. They are awesome.

I drove around the bay and parked my car at an overlook spot. There were no other cars or people around. I got out, walked to a rocky ledge, and stood amidst a bank of wild orange poppies. I could see whales playing in the bay, as well as see small groups of whales swimming past the park, heading out into open water. After a short period of time, the three females in the bay left and followed the procession of whales out to sea. I watched for several minutes as other groups of two or three whales at a time joined the procession. It was now late in the afternoon. I was feeling a need to leave and go home because Nina and I were having a meditation group meeting at our home that evening. I wanted to help her prepare for it, but I was so thrilled at seeing the whales that I lingered a big longer.

Just then I saw a larger group of orcas swim around the point by the park, and head straight toward me. When they first surfaced to breathe, they were in an uneven line; I counted seven whales. The number seven is my special number. I watched intently as they swam toward me, and the next time they came up to breathe they were getting into a straight line.

Then the most incredible thing happened. When the seven whales were right in front of me, close to the rocky outcropping where I was standing, they all arched up completely out of the water in a perfectly synchronized leap. Nose to nose in a precisely straight line, they looked like a perfectly-rehearsed chorus line in a graceful ballet. It was exquisite. They came completely out of the water in front of me and then gracefully went back down into the water, in unison. After they went back down into the water, two of them came right back up, side by side, and waved their tales at me! It was a playful acknowledgment of my presence, and I felt a deep communication between us. Then they swam out to join the procession with the other whales.

I stood there on the ledge, transfixed, crying and laughing, then jumping up and down, feeling absolutely ecstatic. I thanked the orcas profusely for welcoming me to the island, and I said to myself out loud, "I'm home, I'm home!" It was one of the most incredible experiences of my life, for which I am deeply grateful.

I have seen the orcas many times since that day, and it is always a thrill. I have been out on friends' boats and on whale-watch cruises several times when the whales have come up to the boat, sometimes swimming under the boat, and usually being very playful. It always feels profound to me. And sometimes the whales pay no attention to us as they are busy feeding or purposefully swimming somewhere. There have been times when I have been out on the rocks at Whale Watch Park when groups of children are present. The orcas seem particularly drawn to children. I watch the children responding to the whales, and the kids often look transformed when the orcas come up close to the rocks and acknowledge them.

As spring unfolded, it was clear that I would not have enough island clients to support me financially. Again I looked in the newspaper—the local island newspaper this time—and saw an ad for a part-time typesetter. I had no experience in typesetting, but since I was an excellent typist I decided to apply and find out if they would train me. The owner of the printing shop interviewed me. I really liked her, and she could have trained me for her business. But then she told me that the County Public Works Department was desperately looking for a secretary. She seemed inspired to call and arrange an interview for me the next day at Public Works.

It was a simple, small, informal office, very different from the research center in Seattle, but I liked the feeling in the office and the friendliness of the employees. The office supervisor needed a secretary right away so that she could take the two-week trip she had planned, for which she would be leaving in a couple of weeks. I agreed to start right away and work part-time on a temporary basis, so that she could train me to handle the office while she was absent. I think I started the next day. It didn't seem to matter that I was sixty-three years old. I had computer skills that I developed at the research center, and for these I was grateful.

It was such a different office environment for me. I was mostly working with engineers and members of the road crew that maintained the roads and docks on all of the islands in the county. They were an informal and jovial group, and I really enjoyed working with the guys. The islanders from the various islands in the county who called in by phone were also extremely friendly. Part of my duties was to greet the people who came in and to answer the phone. I loved the small town atmosphere and the warm manner in which they welcomed a newcomer. I was a bit overwhelmed, however, when my supervisor left, putting me in charge of the office. Everybody pitched in and helped me when I needed it, but it definitely stretched me.

When my supervisor returned, she said she had to immediately begin the process of hiring a full time secretary. I had told her earlier that I was not interested in working full time. During her absence, though, I came to truly enjoy the office and the other employees. It was challenging but fun. I knew it would not be easy for me to work full time and also be available for the energy work, but it felt right to take on the challenge, and I needed the income. So I applied for the position, took the secretarial tests, passed them, and was hired.

I had a lot to learn, and I needed some time to adjust to working full time, but everyone was very helpful and appreciative of my efforts. It was a great way to get acquainted with the islanders because so many people came into the office. In addition to all the contractors, surveyors, and other public works employees, I met many of the county public officials. One of my responsibilities was to take our mail for other county employees to the county courthouse in town every day and to distribute it in the appropriate boxes. I got acquainted with many people in the courthouse that way. Friday Harbor is a friendly town, and there are many fascinating people who live on these islands.

Shortly after I began working full time at Public Works, some new and special friends on the island needed a house sitter for about a five-week period. They had planned an extended trip with their young daughter and needed someone to take care of their dogs, cats, and the gardens. I had never been a house sitter before, but Nina had several guests coming in during the summer period, and I wanted to help my friends. Besides that, I was longing to live away from town and closer to nature. Nina's home was right in town on a busy street.

I loved being in this home. It was located in a wooded area in the central part of the island. So instead of sounds of traffic I heard the sounds of a variety of birds. It was beautiful. The next thing I learned was that news travels rapidly on the island, and soon I was called for another house-sitting job in a different part of the island with a south view of the water. Nina was thinking of moving to an apartment, so I put my things in a storage locker and accepted the second house-sitting job for about a month. While I was there I got a call from a couple who needed a house sitter for four months while they were gone to Australia for the winter. They wouldn't be back until mid-March. I accepted, and I began my third house-sitting job which was in a magnificent large home built high on a bluff, overlooking the west shore of the island. It had an incredible view, and I regularly saw eagles, deer, rabbits and many other wondrous creatures. This home was only a fifteen-minute drive from Public Works. Once again I was so beautifully provided for.

Meanwhile, during the summer I learned about a large local community choral group called the San Juan Singers. I had not had the opportunity of singing with a choral group since my husband and I sold our home in Minneapolis and moved into the Castle Community when I was about forty. Prior to that I was singing in a large chorus called The Bach Society Chorale in Minneapolis. It was an excellent choral group. Since our rehearsal room was near the University of Minnesota and we had an outstanding director, we were the chorus that was usually called upon when the Minnesota Orchestra performed a symphonic piece that required a chorus. Robert Shaw was the guest conductor for this concert, which was performed in the Symphony Hall. We rehearsed with him for three nights, and then performed three evening concerts. It was an exhausting week, but exhilarating beyond belief. By the end of those concerts, I think most of us would have died for Robert Shaw. He was as beautiful a person as he was a phenomenal conductor.

I auditioned at the first fall rehearsal of the San Juan Singers and was accepted. Literally, my heart sang too, because I was so thrilled to again be able to participate in a musical endeavor, singing with the San Juan Singers in Friday Harbor. The chorus consisted of about fifty singers and we, too, had an excellent director. I sang for several years with the Singers, and also for about five years with a small group called Sotto Voce. In this smaller group, most of us were part of the Singers as well. We sang Renaissance music in Latin and a cappella. I loved that music. It deeply resonated with my soul.

The Singers concerts are held in our Community Theatre in town. It is quite an extraordinary theatre for a small island community. It seats about 300 people and was built and dedicated just shortly before I moved here fourteen years ago. Many performers from around the country, and the world, put on concerts here. Our well-equipped stage accommodates dramas and musicals of all kinds. There is an outstanding drama and theater program for all ages, so children, teens, as well as adults, have many opportunities to perform.

Without exception, the most profound experience I have ever had with music occurred during a concert with the San Juan Singers my second year in the chorus. For the Christmas concert that year our featured choral work was a beautiful Mass in Latin composed by Giacomo Puccini. It was an extremely challenging piece of music for our group of fifty-five singers, and we had worked hard to learn the music and perform it to our director's satisfaction. During our dress rehearsal of the concert, our singing of the Mass was the best performance we had attained. It was just marvelous. I am commonly inspired and deeply moved emotionally and spiritually by beautiful music. However, early into the Mass I began to feel something I had never experienced before. I simply blended with the music and became one with it. It was very different from feeling deeply inspired by the music. I WAS the music. There was no separation. It was an absolutely phenomenal experience for me.

The next night at our opening concert, our choral group was expecting another exemplary performance. However, early into the Mass one of the soloists missed a cue and came in one beat off. Our director appeared to be scrambling a bit to get us all back on the same beat and into the flow. In spite of her efforts, I sensed some hesitation and uncertainty among the singers, and our performance of the Mass was not inspired as it had been the night before. Still, I slipped into the same experience of oneness with the music as I had the previous night. I was totally aware of both those moments, when we were singing sublimely and when we made mistakes, and it did not matter. There was no judgment. The feeling of being blended, at one with the music, was not at all related to the perfection of our performance. I felt incredibly joyous in both performances. It was a spectacular lesson for me. I learned that oneness is our natural state of being when we can let go of judgments.

The owners of the mansion, where I had been house-sitting for four months, returned in mid-March as planned. I had been looking at the local newspaper's want ads for a place to rent, but my guidance said, "Don't call—trust." I felt awkward and somewhat embarrassed about not having a home, but I had to follow what felt right. After all, I had been trusting my spiritual guidance for a long time, and it had always proven to be trustworthy. I stayed temporarily with a friend. And then some other friends—a wonderful couple—invited me to rent a furnished double-wide mobile home on their property fairly close to their home. I moved there in April.

It was situated on a beautiful thirty-acre setting, pristine land, quiet and serene, with a gorgeous view of the Olympic Mountains.

Daily I could watch deer, rabbit, quail families, and lots of birds right outside my windows. I learned so much about their patterns, their individual habits and family interactions. The baby bunnies were adorable. Three does had babies that spring, with one set of twins. A yearling male was getting his first antlers, all fuzzy and about six inches long. The animals were not afraid of me, and if I moved slowly and talked softly to them, I could get fairly close to them. My friends and I all lived simply and harmoniously with the earth. Much energy work could be accomplished there because the land is so pure and love is so abundant. I lived there until early November. At that point the water pipes had to be drained and the house closed up for the winter. Once again, the couple who owned the magnificent big house where I had lived the previous winter asked me to housesit while they were in Australia, and I moved to that home directly. All was in divine order once again.

All of this time I was working at Public Works, but I had earned vacation time. That year I took two wonderful trips. The first one was to Maui for ten days in January. My daughter, Sharon, and her boyfriend were living on Maui and I stayed with them. We had a precious time together, highlighted by a walk with Sharon into the crater of Mount Haleakala, where the energies I was carrying from San Juan Island were released and grounded. (My spiritual guides were in charge of that energy work.) We also had a great weekend exploring the Big Island.

Then in September I flew to Minnesota for eight days to be with my son, Grant, and his wife, Raenay, who had just had their first baby, a beautiful little girl named Haeley. I also saw my daughter, Susan and her son, Deon, now age five. Over the next few years, Grant and Raenay would have a baby boy named Erick, and Susan would have a baby girl named Alana. That makes four grandchildren, all living in Minneapolis. Though I love living on this island, and I know that I am to be here, I have missed seeing my grandchildren grow up. They are all bright and wonderful kids. But in this lifetime it has not been my purpose to live near my grandchildren and be a closely involved grandmother, as so many others are. Sometimes

I feel sad about that. I go back to see them once a year usually, and it is a joyous time to renew my ties to my children, grandchildren, and long-time friends. Grant and his family have come to visit me on the island a few times, and Sharon has been here a great many times.

A few months after I had my sixty-fifth birthday I decided it was time to retire. It had become too stressful for me to work fulltime, and there was no opportunity to work in that job on a part-time basis. The staff put on a surprise retirement party for me, which was delightful and heart-touching. I had worked there for two years, and in many ways I felt sad about leaving. Soon after retiring I was introduced to a couple who had a small business in town and who needed some temporary part-time help in their office. That was my next work experience. There I was introduced to two other men who were entrepreneurs on the island, and each of them had their offices set up in their homes. They needed secretarial help, and I worked for each of them on a small part-time basis. There are many creative people who live on this island. Many run successful businesses out of their homes. In fact, the creativity on this island is phenomenal. There are artists, writers, musicians, and practitioners of all kinds engaged in a variety of healing arts. Many spiritually-motivated people have been drawn to this island, as I was. There are meditation groups and workshops being presented frequently.

Within a few months after my retirement from Public Works, a new small apartment complex was built on the outskirts of town. I applied for an apartment while it was still under construction, and I moved in as soon as it was completed and open for occupancy. I loved my apartment. All of the buildings are single-story, and my apartment was on the end with a southeast exposure. I had a great deal of privacy and it overlooked a lovely eight-acre meadow, with many trees clustered around it. I had abundant space for flower gardens, and I loved my flowers. Even though it was in town, it was wonderfully quiet. Not only was it at the end of a dead-end street, it was far enough from the busy part of the town so that I could see the dazzling night sky without interference of street lights. I saw many kinds of birds, a deer or two in the meadow now and then, and sometimes eagles soaring overhead. I had lovely neighbors, too. This definitely felt like home, and once again my needs were provided for. Because of its location, a lot of energy work was accomplished there. A huge granite rock sat about twenty-five feet from the front of my apartment. It had a naturally-carved face on which I saw two eyes, a nose, and a very comical crooked grin. I grinned every time I looked at it. That rock assisted in grounding the energy that was focused there.

Not long after I moved to my new apartment, I received a call from a dear island friend in which she told me that she and her fiancé had decided to get married. She wanted to let me know the date so that hopefully I could join them at their wedding. As she talked about their wedding plans, it appeared that all of their plans had quite easily fallen into place except for finding a minister. The couple wanted to be married in a small airplane, flying over the islands. The ministers they had contacted either did not call back or were not interested in officiating.

I thought it was a lovely idea to be married in an airplane, flying over the islands. So I told her if she got stuck and couldn't find a minister that I was ordained and legally could marry them. She was elated, though surprised when I told her, for she did not know that I was an ordained minister. Actually, I don't think I had told anybody on the island. It just never came up because I was not conducting any services that required ordination. I also told her that I had never performed a marriage ceremony, so I would have to find out what I needed to do. They did not care that it was my first wedding. I called Dorothy Sinclair in Seattle, who had ordained me about ten years previously. I knew that she had performed hundreds of weddings in their lovely chapel over a long period of time. Dorothy was great. She sent me a couple of her basic ceremonies and instructed me in the procedure for filling out the legal documents. I met with my friends, who had found a couple of sample marriage ceremonies, and together we created the ceremony that felt perfect for them.

The wedding was on a beautiful sunny day on the Memorial Day weekend. The law requires that two witnesses be present in addition to the bride, groom, and minister. The couple reserved a six-seater plane with pilot, and the three of us, plus the maid of honor and the best man, all boarded the plane. The maid of honor was a naturalist on a whale-watch boat. She had called the whale resource center before we boarded the plane to find out where the whales had been sighted recently. The pilot flew us over that area of the sea, and there they were. It was my first time to see the orca whales from the air. What a thrill for all of us. We flew over a couple of other islands, and as we approached Mount Constitution on Orcas Island, the bride and groom told me they were ready. It was high noon. We then proceeded with the ceremony. The bride and groom sat in the center two seats, the best man sat in the front next to the pilot, and the maid of honor sat next to me in the back row. I leaned forward, and the bride and groom faced each other. As I read the ceremony and they said their vows, we had to talk loudly because of the noise in the airplane, but it all flowed beautifully. The marriage was accomplished, and it felt magical to all of us.

Following the marriage ceremony, there was a reception planned in a beautiful home located near the highest point on the island. Most of the wedding guests were gathered outside on the deck of that home, awaiting the arrival of the bride and groom following their marriage ceremony in the airplane. With the ceremony completed, the pilot flew us over the home and tipped his wings. This had been planned ahead, and the guests, who were expecting to see us, waved wildly at us. It was such fun for everyone. After the plane landed at the airport, the five of us drove to the home for the reception. Since all of the guests, except for the attendants, would not have witnessed the ceremony, the bride and groom and I had prepared another ceremony especially for them. They did not make their wedding vows again, but it was a beautiful ceremony, that included the bride and groom singing to each other, and a few guests reading special selections.

During the reception, several people complimented me on the ceremony. When I responded by saying it was my first wedding, they asked me why I was not doing this regularly. They said I was a natural for it. The whole process had been such a joyous and magical experience that I asked myself, "Why am I not doing this?" Before the evening was over, I had decided to go for it. One of the guests gave me some suggestions about how to get started. It seemed the first step would be to create a business card that I could distribute in town. An artist friend helped me design the card, and I had the cards printed. They were quite beautiful. I first took them to the auditor's office in the court house where they issue the marriage licenses.

I already knew most of the people that worked there. I also gave them to florists, caterers, photographers, inn keepers, resort personnel, and friends who had contacts. Before long I was receiving phone calls from couples planning to get married.

Meanwhile, I had written three sample ceremonies that I could make available to couples. I borrowed some portions from Dorothy's ceremonies and other sources, and incorporated many of my own thoughts. It was very important to me that the words I spoke at each wedding would be meaningful to that particular couple, recognizing that every one is different, and what is meaningful to one couple may not be meaningful to another couple. My ceremonies included one that was a fairly traditional Christian ceremony, one that was more spiritual, and another one that could be considered a civil ceremony. All of them contained thoughts that I felt were beautiful sentiments about love, marriage, and relationships. I encouraged every couple to write their own ceremony. Most of them said they did not know where to start, so I offered my ceremonies as a resource.

In the summer and fall I officiated at several weddings. Each was very different, and each was beautiful and heart-warming. I totally enjoyed each wedding. One was in a chapel, one out on the lawn at a B&B, and the others in homes, gardens, or in various beautiful places in nature. This, too, was variety, and I thrive on variety. Over the ensuing years I created two more wedding ceremonies, for a total of five, which I send to each couple if they want them. Some couples choose one of my ceremonies, but the majority write their own. Often they incorporate various portions from different ceremonies I send them, thereby creating a ceremony that expresses what is in their hearts and minds on this precious and significant moment in their lives. I have never chosen for any couple what I say in their marriage ceremony. The whole process is exciting and fun for me. I love to hear each couple's story: their background, how they met, and their dreams for the future.

I was thrilled to have these inspiring events in my life, and it was a new source of income. A friend helped me design a web page for my wedding services, and over the years I have continued to officiate at many weddings. The last time I counted I had performed several hundred weddings. Couples come here from all over the country to get married, and I have had a few weddings for couples who have come here from other countries. As I am writing this, that first wedding couple is still happily married. They recently celebrated their tenth anniversary, and they still live on the island.

Early that first year I had two couples ask me if I had a robe to wear. Up to that point I had been wearing one of two dresses that I thought were appropriate. But I discovered that many couples prefer to have the minister be dressed in a robe, so I ordered a robe to be made for me. It is a simple design in a beautiful color of medium blue. Besides being quite lovely, the robe is very comfortable, and I wear it for most weddings. Occasionally a couple will ask me to dress casually, especially if we are in a boat. I have had many weddings in small boats, large yachts, and on beaches. Lots of couples choose a beautiful setting in a park or in the woods. However, I have never had another wedding in an airplane. Some are formal and elaborate events, especially those at resorts or in churches, but more often they are semi-formal or casual. Many couples elope to the island, and I provide two friends to be their witnesses.

The most unusual wedding call, by far, that I have received was from a man who asked, "Do you marry clowns?" I wondered what on earth he had in mind and responded, "Well, sure, clowns can get married like any one else." He told me that he and his fiancé were professional clowns on the mainland. They wanted to be married on the island, dressed in their clown costumes. They did indeed wear their costumes. I wore my robe, and over it I wore the bride's colorful sleeveless clown vest. They wrote their own ceremony that included many beautiful and loving sentiments, as well as considerable "clowning around." It was held in a public park in town, with many island residents who gathered to watch. That event, with photos, hit the front pages of both island newspapers.

Very recently I officiated at a wonderful wedding for a local couple who are professional deep sea divers. Several of us went out on a beautiful large boat and motored over to one of the nearby islands. Before the ceremony the bride and groom put on all of their diving gear, their suits, flippers, and masks. In addition, the bride put on a multicolored wig and stone-studded tiara over her headgear, and the groom put on a colorful fabric tall hat. They stood before me on the platform for their marriage ceremony, and they exchanged their vows and wedding rings. Right after I pronounced them husband and wife, they embraced, put on their gloves, and then went backward into the water for a deep dive that lasted nearly an hour. We waited for them, of course, and when they came up they still had on their hat, wig and tiara. It was joyous, and I loved it. This wedding reminded me of the airplane wedding, except that I did not go down to the bottom with them.

Two of my weddings were for lesbian couples. Although these marriages could not be legalized because, as of this writing, Washington State does not yet allow it, the ceremonies were beautiful, heart-felt, and happy events. I absolutely support gay rights, and I look forward to the day when gay and lesbian couples can have the same legal marriages as all other couples. I have many close friends who are lesbian or gay. I have anguished with some of them over the discrimination they encounter in so many aspects of their lives, and I know that this discrimination will cease as we begin to experience the transformation of consciousness on our planet.

A few years ago my spiritual guides told me that while I was officiating at each wedding, they were able to focus energies through me for the earth during the marriage ceremony. Because the couple and all of their guests were full of joy, their hearts were open. Therefore, each of them could assist in the energy transmission, even though they were not consciously aware of what was happening. All they knew was that they were happy and feeling good. But they were participating in something significant, and they were helping me carry out my primary purpose in this life. What a magnificent plan Spirit created. It is brilliant!

Another event with a similar purpose occurred when I was approaching my seventieth birthday. Our community theatre was preparing to put on a production of "The Sound of Music." I love that play, and I went to the auditions because I wanted to sing in the Nun's Chorus. I especially love the music that the nuns sing, all of which is in Latin. After the auditions for the Nun's Chorus were completed, the director began to audition for the major roles in the play. I stayed around to watch, sitting with some special friends. When they began the auditions for the role of the Mother Abbess (Mother Superior), I heard my name called. I thought it was a mistake, but my friends told me to stand up and go on stage. So I did. They auditioned several people for that part, including me. I knew The Reverend Mother sang some solos, including "Climb Every Mountain," and I had never sung a solo in my life. I also knew that solo had a fairly high range, and I am an alto. Besides, I had never acted in a play. I assumed they would choose another person.

However, after the auditions were finished for that evening and people were leaving, the music director asked me to come back on stage and sing "Climb Every Mountain." She was a good friend from the San Juan Singers chorus. I protested, but she insisted. Though she helped me, I didn't do very well. She asked me to come back the following night for the final auditions, which I did. Again I read for The Reverend Mother's part, and I was paired off with a young woman who was auditioning for the role of Maria. She was fairly new to the island, and we had not met before, but a strong connection formed between us—a feeling of chemistry which was quite astounding.

All of us were told that decisions would be made about each role within a few days and that we would be notified. A couple of nights later my spiritual guides told me that I would be asked to play the role of The Reverend Mother, and that I must accept it. They said that the poignant scene at the end of act 1, in which The Reverend Mother counsels Maria when she returns to the Abbey after she has fallen in love with the Captain, would be the pivotal point. Because of Maria's anguish about her decision to return to the Abbey, most people in the audience could relate to this and would have their hearts open. I would then sing, "Climb Every Mountain," during which time my guides would focus the energies through me. All of those in the audience who were open would be assisting in the grounding of the energies.

Sure enough, a few days later the director called and asked me to play that role. I did remind her that I had never sung a solo before and had no acting experience, but she definitely wanted me to be The Reverend Mother in the play. It was clearly divinely orchestrated. I accepted, with fear and trembling, and told her I would take voice lessons to prepare. I enjoyed the voice lessons, and I really loved the rehearsals with the other actors. Learning my lines and remembering them, however, was a challenge. Memorizing has never been a strong suit for me. I invited Mother Hildegard from the Benedictine Abbey on our neighboring Shaw Island to come over and teach me how to do the Catholic blessings and how to wear the habit. She counseled all of us nuns in the show. She was delightful, and it was a helpful experience for us.

Maria and Jean

Even though I had done a lot of public speaking and been on stage in choruses innumerable times,

152

this was an unbelievable stretch for me; I had to conquer many fears. I was terrified the first time I had to sing "Climb Every Mountain" with the fourteen-piece orchestra in front of the whole cast. But because I loved playing the role, and because the young woman who played Maria, with whom I felt such an immense connection, was so fantastic, I soon relaxed. It was very natural for us to do those scenes together. The entire cast—the directors, orchestra, stage crew, sound and light people, costumers and make-up people—all became a very bonded and supportive family. We put on eight performances and played to a full house almost every performance. It was a smashing success, and the audiences loved it. And at each performance the energies for the earth were focused and grounded. It was one of the most powerful experiences in my life, and one of the most enjoyable.

So that is how I celebrated my seventieth birthday. What an initiation into my next decade! Actually, it was quite liberating, and I felt confident to take greater risks. Right after the play was over, I launched into the heaviest schedule of weddings I had ever had, and I continued singing in the choral groups. I also loved working in my flower gardens, spending time at the beaches, and being close to nature whenever possible.

Another exciting musical experience for me was to join with some of my island friends and learn how to play the African marimba and a small hand-held instrument called an mbira. The marimbas were made like the original instruments from Zimbabwe, and our local teacher had been trained by a teacher from that country. I bought one of the mbiras made in Zimbabwe, and I often played it in my home. I love this music, and it was great fun to play with the group.

In 2001 I participated in a spiritual workshop on San Juan Island. During a meditation, I was given the answer to my question, which I had asked many years before in that New Years Eve channeling session with Frank Homan, about where I came from. (All I was told then was that I came from a dimension and when the time was right I would remember.) In that meditation I learned that I came from the realm of the archangels. It was an extremely emotional experience for me, and many tears rolled down my cheeks. I felt and saw in my mind my "family," and I was told that I came here to earth in order to be an emissary for them. Then they took me "home" to our dimension. There are no words to describe this experience. It was so ecstatically beautiful that when I came out of the meditation my feelings were similar to what I have heard from others who have had a near-death experience. It was painful to be in my body on the earth plane after being in that other dimension, and I didn't want to be here. When the meditation ended, I went outside alone, and I wept for a long time. I had felt for many years a close tie to the angelic realm, but I was not aware until that experience that I had, in fact, come from there, and it was home for me.

One of the most magical and profound experiences of "Oneness" for me occurred mid-day a few years ago. As I was leaving my apartment and walking down the sidewalk, I noticed ahead of me there was a beautiful monarch butterfly sitting there in the middle of the sidewalk. I stopped and began to talk to it, telling the butterfly how beautiful it was. The butterfly was slowly opening and closing its wings in a rhythmic pattern, and I was fascinated. I stooped down and told the butterfly that I would love to gently touch its wings, but I would understand if it did not want me to do that and chose to fly away.

I slowly moved my right hand down toward the butterfly, and when it closed its wings I very gently stroked them. I moved my hand away, and the butterfly opened its wings again and then slowly closed them. I then stroked its wings again, and we began this beautiful rhythmic dance together. I felt a deep communion of oneness between us as we continued this dance. It was magical and I was deeply moved. Then I became aware of one of my neighbors walking toward me on the sidewalk from the opposite direction. I didn't want this exquisite experience to be interrupted with conversation, so I told the butterfly that this wasn't a good location for us to be together. I said I would very gently pick it up and carry it to a nice grassy place by a tree in my front yard, which is what I did. After I set the butterfly down, my neighbor called out a greeting to me from the sidewalk. I turned briefly to return the greeting to her, and when I looked back at the butterfly, it was gone. It was nowhere in sight. I couldn't imagine how it could have flown away so quickly.

I sat down on the grass alone for a few minutes, savoring the memory and the feeling of our oneness. I felt sad that this profound experience had ended, but I also felt deep joy and gratitude for this blessing.

Not long after that experience, one of my precious island friends called me. She was preparing to go on her first vision quest, and she asked me if she could carry with her the sacred pipe I was given. I was most happy to share the pipe with her, because I knew of her deep commitment to the Native American traditions, to nature and to the earth. We also had done a lot of energy work together over the years. And I remembered my vision quest in Texas many years before, when a Texas friend loaned me the sacred pipe she carried so I could take it with me. I invited my island friend to come to my home one evening to pick up the pipe. I had not felt called to schedule a pipe ceremony for quite some time, and I had not received any requests for a ceremony. I brought my pipe bag out into my living room and sat down in my special chair, holding the pipe on my lap. My friend felt the need to go into meditation, and both of us were aware of intense energy work going on. While she was meditating, I took the sacred pipe out of its special bag and held it. Immediately I was flooded with memories of all my experiences with the pipe over the years. It was as if a video started playing in my mind.

I was then told by my guidance team that it was time for me to pass the sacred pipe on to my friend, not just to loan it to her, for my work with the pipe was completed. I was quite shocked. Suddenly feelings of grief welled up in me. Tears flowed down my cheeks as I said good-bye to the pipe I carried, and then feelings of great joy came up. I knew instinctively that I was finished with this beautiful pipe, and I knew that my friend was the perfect person to whom it should be passed. I began to smile and was eagerly waiting for her to finish her meditation. When she opened her eyes, I asked her if she knew what was to happen next. She said, "No." Then I told her about my guidance and the experience I had just had of completion. I told her that it was time for me to pass the pipe on to her. She looked stunned. Then she told me that part of the reason for her vision quest was that she hoped to receive an answer to her question about whether she was worthy to be a pipe carrier. It amazed her to receive her answer before her vision quest. It was a beautiful experience for both of us, and she gratefully took the pipe with her on her vision quest. Since then I have been to a ceremony that she conducted. It was a special dedication of a friend's teepee, and we all smoked the pipe as it was passed. All was in divine order once again.

I only occasionally work with individual clients now, but the planetary energy work has escalated. Some of those energy transmissions have caused extreme stress in my physical body, especially to my heart. There have been two particular instances in which my body was stretched a bit beyond its limits and I almost left it. In each instance, however, friends were guided to call me or come by to see me and provide healing to assist my body to come back into balance. A couple of times I was taken to our local medical clinic for emergency care when I had an episode of atrial fibrillations.

From my conversations with friends who are committed to their spiritual paths, and especially those of us who work with energies, it seems that all of us have gone through some significant changes and been involved in more intense energy work since the beginning of this new century. We are clearly evolving into the higher dimensions and assisting Mother Earth in her changes.

There are so many precious friends of mine with whom I have participated in energy work for the earth. I could not begin to name them all without unintentionally leaving some out, but I do want to especially thank Mark Gibson, who lives in Seattle. Mark and I have worked together for nearly twenty years now, and also in previous lives on this planet and in the other realms. Many times Spirit has worked through us together, even though we have not been physically in each other's presence. Sometimes this occurs when we are talking on the telephone. On an intellectual level I do not understand how this happens, but I clearly know that the work occurs and that there are no limitations when we are functioning in the other dimensions. Mark has also channeled messages from Sananda and other masters for me on a great number of occasions when I have had physical challenges or questions. I am so grateful for his assistance.

There was a period of time for me in late spring of 2001 when the earth changes were happening so fast and with such intensity that I felt as if I was going through the "dark night of the soul." Then on July 4, on my way home from watching the fireworks with a friend, I was involved in a very minor car accident right in town. Another car hit my right front wheel. Even though I initially did not think I was hurt at all, the accident set into motion a variety of health problems, including muscle spasms in my back, heart fibrillations and, most miserable of all, a case of shingles on my left thigh. I had never had shingles and really didn't know much about the condition. Besides the pain and discomfort of the rash and numbness in my thigh muscle, it totally zapped my energy level, which I later learned from many others is quite typical.

So here I was, in what was normally the busiest time of my year, with almost no energy, and finding it painful to walk. Somehow I managed to carry out the weddings I had scheduled, without appearing impaired. (It was, however, a major challenge for me to put on pantyhose and the other garments.) But I did not have as heavy a schedule as usual, and was being provided for as always. So it was a quiet summer for me, and I spent a great deal of time sleeping and resting. I know that I co-create everything that happens to me, but I could not understand why I had created the shingles in July when I expected to be so busy. My guidance was totally silent (like they all went on vacation), and I did not do a good job of accepting that all of this was in divine order and that there was a purpose for it. I just felt confused and miserable, and, I admit, I whined a lot to my good friends.

It was not until late August that I received my first message from my guidance team. They said, *"We are almost finished with the process you are going through, and soon you will feel much better."* A few days later my guides told me that I had been going through a major transformation once again. They said, *"You are now at another whole level of ability to handle the high frequencies of energy, which will serve you, and us, extremely well in the days and months to come. This period of rest and quietness was necessary to accomplish the goal."* I was very happy to know what had been going on, but later I got angry with my guides about the fact that they and I chose to put me through this process in July and August. Why could I not go through these changes next January and February? Why in the summer?

Early in September I learned about the extraordinary astrological configurations that included the two grand trines forming a Star of David in the heavens during the second and third weeks of September. Then I realized that the personal process of transformation I had just gone through in the summer had to be completed before that time period. It seemed significant that all of this took place before September 11, 2001. I also came to understand why my guidance "went on vacation." It was still another test for me to accept that there are no accidents and that everything serves a purpose. Following September 11th, I was regularly plugged in to various energy projects, including helping to cleanse the grief energy in the world.

The planetary transformation is clearly in process. The earth, all human beings, and all other life forms are going through immense changes because of the necessary alterations in energy frequencies on the planet. It is a very demanding process for all of us, and yet it is exciting.

And now I come to the point where I began my story in Chapter 1, in which I said that I had been guided and connected with many others in order to create a new spiritual center in Costa Rica for the transformation of consciousness on our planet. The Costa Rica project began early in 2003 when friends learned of an exquisite piece of property in the mountains of Costa Rica that was for sale. One of them, who was there on the land, had a vision of a large octagonal-shaped building that was to stand on a high knoll with a 360-degree view of the property and surrounding area.

This is sacred land, a repository of artifacts from a civilization that dates back to pre-Columbian times. There are seven year-round springs that cross the land and three waterfalls on the property. The largest waterfall is about twenty-five feet high and is exquisitely beautiful. The land is situated in the most natural greenhouse in all of Costa Rica at an elevation of 3,900 feet, with a year-round temperature of about seventy-one degrees. The Java River borders the west side of the property, and just across the river is the world-famous Wilson Botanical Gardens property.

A core group of people were drawn together, directed by spiritual guidance, to create a center on that spot for the transformation of consciousness. Some of my close friends were part of this group. I was one of the first to volunteer to participate in this project and help to fulfill this vision. My guidance did not tell me that—I just had a deep knowing within me. The eighty-three acres were purchased by two of the people in the group. The name of the new Center is "Gardens of Heaven—Costa Rica."

A beautiful brochure was created and states our purpose: "Part of the overall program for this Center will be directed toward transforming human consciousness from an Ego-centered consciousness to an Eco-centered consciousness, honoring Nature and Spirit in each unfolding manifestation. This will be a Center where people may come for personal retreat or healing, and for small and large group gatherings to enhance the discovery, awakening, and activation of creativity. It will be a place to experience a new sense of peace, love, joy, aliveness, and community, all in harmony with nature and an expanding spiritual vision. A place where people may experience oneness with all of creation."

In June 2004 three others in the group and I went to Costa Rica and spent time on the property during the summer solstice. Two of them had been there before, but it was my first visit. On the summer solstice I was on that sacred knoll, and powerful energies were focused through me and grounded. It was an incredible experience for me. I was given the message from my spiritual guides that I had been on that land before, eons ago, and I had made a commitment to come back at this time period to re-activate the spiritual energy in order to facilitate the transformation of consciousness on our planet. It was accomplished. The higher frequencies were definitely grounded on that knoll. My body was stressed and took a few hours to feel rebalanced again, but I felt fine later on.

I loved Costa Rica. I loved the people, the culture, the music, the exquisite beauty of the land, the flowers and trees, birds and butterflies, and the weather. Costa Rica is a democratic country, and voting is important to everyone. Free transportation is provided for those who need it in order to get to their polling place. They have no military program, and they have excellent health care and educational systems. While we were at our property, we stayed with a retired American couple who owned property adjacent to our eighty-three acres. They were very friendly and hospitable. It was a joy and privilege to be with them and to have easy access to our property. We also stayed for three days with a Costa Rican family that live in a suburb of San Jose. Everyone was so friendly, and included us in all the festivities. We were present for a birthday party for the "grandma." My heart was deeply touched by their loving extended family. The grandchildren were just a delight, and I became aware of the difference in the meaning of "family" in Costa Rica. The respectfulness that flowed between the adults to the children and the children to the adults was at a level that I have rarely observed in our country, and the interactions between the young grandchildren were beautiful to behold. It was a totally joyful time, with lots of music and singing. And I absolutely loved their food.

One memory is forever etched in my mind. Our Costa Rican host was driving us from San Jose through the mountains to our property in the southern part of the country. We climbed to an altitude of over 11,000 feet. I was sitting in the front passenger seat, talking with our driver, when suddenly as I was looking to the left I saw the Caribbean Sea stretching to infinity. It was an awesome view. A few moments later I glanced out my window to the right, and there was the Pacific Ocean. It was incredible to be driving along a ridge that allowed us to view both oceans. I doubt that there are many places on our continent where such a view is available.

Our group anticipated that adequate funds would be acquired to enable us to develop the property and build the necessary facilities. That has not happened yet, and it will be an enormous undertaking. However, it may turn out that the anchoring of that high frequency energy in that strategic spot, and the protection of the property from commercial development, was the ultimate purpose at this time for the purchase of that sacred land. We don't know yet, but we have no doubt that it will all unfold in divine order.

Chapter 7

Looking Back—Looking Forward

Looking back over my lifetime, I realize not only the divine orchestration of the events in my life experience, but also the enormous changes that have occurred in the United States and around the world during this time period. Born shortly before the Great Depression, I remember how my extended family of parents, grandparents, and great aunts and uncles grouped together to, quite literally, survive. My grandparents had previously been wealthy and lived in a gorgeous big home. Apparently they lost most of their wealth when the stock market crashed in 1929. It must have been a huge adjustment for them to live in a small bungalow, while providing for many brothers and sisters. But, from my childhood perspective, they all seemed to be living harmoniously. Obviously, they had no choice in order to survive, but I think they clearly made the best of a serious situation.

Then the Second World War began. Prior to that time, all the mothers I knew stayed at home to raise their children. But with the crisis of the war, and so many men being called into the armed services, many women went to work in munitions factories and in other areas of business. "Rosie, the Riveter" emerged, giving birth to a new era in which it would be common for women to work. My mother did not go to work, but my father worked in the Ford Motor assembly plant in St. Paul. He worked in the glass department. During the war there were very few, if any, cars or appliances being built. I do not think there was much, if any, home construction either. The manufacturing plants were converted into facilities to produce munitions, tanks, and other materials for the war. Employment opportunities were plentiful. People worked hard and earned money, but there was not much to buy with their income. Butter, meat, gas for automobiles, and all kinds of commodities were rationed. I remember a time when I was in high school that I had a date with a nice boy whose family allowed him to use the family car to take me to the movies. That was a big deal.

Then the United States dropped the atomic bomb on Hiroshima and Nagasaki in Japan. I remember feeling enormously shocked to learn of all the deaths and suffering that resulted, as well as the deaths of some of the young men from our church who were drafted and sent to Europe and Asia. I was in high school at the time. Then I learned about the Holocaust in Germany and the millions of people who died in concentration camps. All of this horrified me.

After the war had ended, the factories returned to manufacturing cars and appliances. I think people had money then, and though lots of people I knew bought new cars, my parents did not. New roads were constructed, and people built homes in the suburban areas on land that once supported family farms. The whole landscape changed, giving rise to the suburban sprawl we see today. It was the birth of a new era in this country. New technologies sprang up everywhere. I remember when I saw my first television set. It was in a lounge at the college, it had a small screen and was in a huge cabinet. I had graduated from high school in 1946, and I was then a nineteen-year-old freshman in college. It would be many years later that the first computers would be available for average people to buy. And then would come photocopy machines, portable telephones, and so many other appliances and gadgets that are now commonplace in our society.

So it has been a fascinating era in which to be alive and to witness great changes in our country and the world. I have also been witness to, and a part of, the emerging of civil rights and women's rights in our country. As I have written earlier in this story, I was very active in the civil rights movement, women's rights movement, protesting the war in Vietnam and working for disarmament.

The incredible value in becoming an elder is that I can look back and see how the patterns in my life in each case have provided the experiences needed to prepare me for the next step in carrying out my life purpose in this embodiment. I truly know that there have been no mistakes, that I have been carefully guided and tenderly cared for by my spiritual guidance team in the other dimensions from which I came. I now know that there are no accidents. This is true even when an event appears to be tragic.

After my divorce from Austin, it was always my desire and expectation that I would marry again, and this man would share my commitment to following my spiritual path. My vision was that we would work together and accomplish much more than I could as a single person. My ultimate dream was that, as a couple, we would also be part of a community dedicated to a spiritual purpose. That never happened. Over many years I dated several nice men, and I had three deep relationships with men whom I loved and respected. One of them introduced me to cross-country skiing, which I loved. I bought skis, boots, and poles, and I continued skiing every winter while I lived in Minnesota. With another I went on a fantastic river rafting adventure. Later, I remembered past lives I had experienced with each of these men. And, in each case, the man whom I loved and who loved me, terminated our relationship. One of them said to me, "Jean, it's not you. I'm just not ready for you." I was very hurt and did not understand at the time what he meant. Each of these men were kind, caring, and spiritual, and I think each of them knew somewhere within themselves that I needed to be free to follow my path. Each time it was a painful experience for me, for my dream was to fulfill my purpose with a loving partner with whom I could share the excitement, the hard times, the joys, and the fulfillment of our spiritual paths together.

I have always been open to connecting with such a man, and in my prayers I have asked for it innumerable times. I could not understand why it did not happen because I felt so much more could be accomplished with both of us working together. I must admit that there were times when I felt punished and deprived. It has only been in the last three or four years (I guess I'm a slow learner in this department) that I have fully realized what was required of me to carry out my purpose, and accepted the fact that my particular role—as being a person through whom very high frequency energies could be focused for our Earth—could not be accomplished if I were in a committed and sexual relationship. At long last I have made peace with this, even though it has often been a lonely road.

Obviously, to carry out my purpose this time, I needed to be free to move about the country as required, as well as to be able to stop and be alone and quiet when the energies needed to be focused through me. No matter how loving and committed a partner or husband would be, that certainly would have been a stressful and demanding challenge for any relationship. And, in order to nurture the relationship, I might not have fulfilled my ultimate commitment and purpose in my life.

One gifted spiritual counselor once told me that I had actually lived two lives in this embodiment. First I was allowed a marriage and having children, which I always fervently wanted, and then, when the time was right, the marriage had to end so that I could fulfill my ultimate purpose and commitment. She even saw a different colored aura around me for each of the two segments of my life.

Austin and I have remained friends throughout these years, and it has been a blessing for my children and myself that we could do that. Even though I have not had the joy of a partner over these past thirty years, I have always received loving comfort and caring from innumerable precious friends. There have also been many people in my life with whom I could play and have fun, and share adventures. Many of these friends have been married couples, but a sizable number of these friends have been without partners and, in many cases, have also longed for a partner.

Now, looking back over these many years, I can clearly see the necessity and wisdom of my being alone. In recent years I have come to appreciate the fact that I live alone. Living alone has given me freedom. It has been a comfort and joy to be able to spontaneously play, meditate, rest, eat what I want when I want it, have silence when I want it, and make choices independently.

Over these past thirty-plus years I have never had financial abundance. Most of the time I have had a small surplus beyond what I needed in order to pay immediate bills, but I have not had a substantial cushion. In financial terms, I have lived my life on faith. As I have written earlier in this book, my spiritual guides have told me that my needs would always be provided for, and that has always been true. I have never been destitute, and for this I am grateful. However, I have often dreamed about financial abundance. Not so that I could have a fancy home, travel, and dress in fine clothes, but rather so I could have a cushion to alleviate my fears around money and to be able to support the causes which are dear to my heart. Having grown up during the Great Depression, I was greatly impacted by my parents' fears of survival. My husband grew up in the same era, of course, and he, too, would worry about money shortages. One of the biggest challenges for me over the past thirty years or so has been to release that fear. It still comes up for me on extremely rare occasions, but most of the time I really know that my needs will continue to be provided for.

The other side of this is that I have come to treasure the simplicity of my life. I have been living in a one-bedroom apartment for eleven years, and it is perfectly adequate for my needs. Earlier in my life I have lived in mansions, but I have no desire at all to live that way now. The only time I wish I had more room is when I have guests. It would be lovely to offer my family and friends a separate and spacious bedroom. But when I think about all the homeless and impoverished people in the world, I feel abundant and well provided for. And besides, my family, friends, and I always have a great time in my little home. I "feel" abundant. My life is still an adventure, I feel in harmony with my purpose, I am doing what I love to do, without fear of the future, and I am supported by loving friends and family. For me, this is true abundance—the real wealth that matters. Also, I'm now very aware that it has been my destiny to live simply and to treasure the simplicity.

When I was in my mid-twenties my husband and I made a brief trip to Havana, Cuba, while we were sightseeing in Miami. This was in the early 1950s before Castro took over. The contrast between the haves and the have-nots was extreme. Our sightseeing bus took us down some roads where we saw an entire family in a small wagon being pulled by a donkey. You could tell that all of their possessions were piled in that wagon. Then we would see very fancy and expensive cars passing them. This poverty was evident in many places. By contrast, we went on a nightclub tour that evening. At the Tropicana nightclub we watched wealthy, elegantly-dressed Cuban men gambling in the casino, throwing large quantities of cash on the tables. This was an eye-opener for me, and it made a lasting impression. I knew then that changes had to happen to narrow the gap between the very wealthy and the poor. I have seen that gap get larger and larger over the years in our country as well.

The older I have gotten, the more grateful I am for everything in my life. A few years ago a friend sent me a beautiful e-mail story about a spiritual teacher who taught everyone to say many times a day: "Thank you for everything. I have no complaints whatsoever." I have discovered that if I repeat that a few times when I'm annoyed, disappointed, anxious, or in pain, I rapidly feel peaceful, relaxed, and happy. It's quite amazing. All day long I am aware of my gratitude for all the blessings in my life, and I often find myself spontaneously saying "thank you" throughout the day, often out loud to myself. Being grateful for what we have is the secret.

I am grateful for the exquisite beauty in nature on this island that nourishes my spirit; the orca whales and other wildlife with which I feel such a close affinity; the fabulous farmers' market filled with gorgeous locally-grown organic produce and meat; my home and flower gardens; my wonderful and loving friends; all of the interesting and growth-enhancing activities here; the challenges in my life, for they help me to grow; and the list goes on. My life has been rich beyond measure.

I give thanks often to God, Creator Source, for helping me bring more love into my heart and for helping assist me to "see" through my heart and not my mind. My mind, my intellect, is a valuable tool, but I want my heart to guide my actions. When I have a problem, I try to surround that problem with love, and give thanks in advance for the perfect resolution of that problem. I know that judgment, of myself and of others, gets in the way of loving, so I give thanks for help in releasing judgments. I strive for an attitude of reverence for all life, for I truly know that we are all one. I have experienced that knowing many times, and it is real. Feeling my oneness with another person, tree, butterfly, mountain, music, or other life form, is bliss.

In 2000 I participated with several friends in a workshop conducted by Dorothy Maclean. Dorothy, back in the 1960s, co-founded, with Peter and

Eileen Caddy, the well-known Findhorn community and garden in Northern Scotland. She learned how to communicate with the angelic kingdom and nature spirits, the results of which are the extraordinary and world-renowned Findhorn garden. I learned from Dorothy how, when we are in a situation where we want a certain outcome and we have done all that we can do, to simply let go and say, "Let love come in." During that same year I read *Conversations With God* and *Friendship With God* by Neale Donald Walsh. I learned from Walsh that when we have to make a difficult decision or choice, and we are not sure which way to go, to ask "What would love do?" I realized that these two approaches are like the two sides of a coin. The first is an allowing, a "surrender," and the second is a "doing," an action. That awareness was powerful and has been very helpful to me in living my life.

I have learned to trust my intuition, my own inner sense about things. Over the past twenty-five years I have received many channeled written messages in which I have been given guidance and awareness about a wide variety of things from my spiritual teachers, angels, and spirit guides. I treasure those messages, those teachings. In recent months, however, I have received only a few written messages from my spiritual guides. Rather, I have a deep knowing within me about things. Perhaps this is the next level. I am not sure.

As I look forward, I truly know that our planet has experienced a shift in the energies that will create a transformation of consciousness among all people—if we will allow it. It may take some time for this to manifest in a tangible manner on the planet, but we are in the process, and it is very exciting. Everything is energy, Spirit is energy, everything is at a frequency of energy. The frequency of energies on the Earth is rising and expanding, and it has been rising in gradual increments over many years. In a real sense, my body has gone through the process of allowing higher and higher levels of frequency of energy to be focused through it. And I believe this is the process that is now taking place on earth.

A few years ago, while I was flying back to Minneapolis to visit my family and friends, the captain of this large aircraft told us that there was a major electrical storm centered over Minneapolis at that time, and the airport was temporarily closed. He said we would be flying in a circle north of Minneapolis until the storm had passed, at which time the airport would be re-opened and we could land. I had a window seat, and it was fascinating to watch the storm in the distance. Then the most incredible sight came into view. Outside my window, I saw a vivid and magnificent rainbow—and the rainbow was round. It was a circle! For an instant I doubted my perception, but then I heard others in the plane exclaiming to their seat-mates that there was a round rainbow out there. I had never heard of this phenomenon; we always see the rainbow as a half-circle when we are on the land or sea.

That round rainbow lasted for a substantial period of time. I have always loved rainbows and been in awe of the beauty of those radiant and luminous colors. For ages the rainbow has been a symbol of transformation for many people. And here was a round rainbow. That stunning vision was for me a magnificent symbol of the transformation I envision taking place on this earth. A vision of people all over the world committed to living in harmony with all life on the earth, honoring all other people, the trees, water, animals, birds, fish, insects, the earth herself—all of life. A vision of people valuing integrity and committed to serving the earth and the common good of all. A vision of recognizing our oneness, and choosing to live in peace and harmony. All of us have a piece of the action in accomplishing this vision.

When I think of this vision, I am reminded of a message that a good friend, who was a very gifted channel and spiritual counselor, was given for me while she was working with me in the early 1980s. The following is an excerpt of this message from a spiritual being who identified herself as Amara from Venus:

Life on Venus is very simple in comparison with how you human beings on earth live out your lives. There is much you could learn from us, for we have learned a simplicity of approach to life situations and we know nothing of the stress that is commonplace among people on your planet. Your preoccupation with material things consumes your time and energy to the detriment of your ability to interact with each other on a soul level.

If you could reduce your needs for material things, you could spend more of your time and energy in communion with the Creator and in joyous pursuits with one another. We look with sorrow upon what seems to us such wasted use of energy and time, when to do such is not necessary. Life need not be filled with so many details. They consume most people on your planet, and they forget what the real purpose of their being is about. Many souls on your planet yearn for a simpler life, and they don't seem to be aware that it is entirely possible, even in your large metropolitan areas.

We wish you to know that we send much loving thoughts and energies to you, and we wish to be helpful, however we may do that, to assist in the evolution on your planet.

Looking ahead, I truly believe we have begun the process of transformation in consciousness on the Earth. And we must.

Many people's dreams include the accumulation of material wealth in order to feel secure, having money in the bank for their retirement, the ability to "buy" what they want, take the trips they want, and to appear "successful" to others. In the process we are consuming ourselves into extinction. As human beings we must shift our focus from marketing, consumerism, and the pursuit of money to caring, first and foremost, about our environment, our natural resources, and all others on the earth. We must focus on preserving our forests and refuse to continue to pollute the air and all of our water sources. We must transform our ideas about the great American dream. If we fail this, our beautiful earth will no longer be able to sustain life, including—and especially—human beings.

We have to preserve the trees, for they absorb the carbon dioxide that the cars and various industries spew into the air. Enormous amounts of mercury have been released into the air through industrial smokestacks and, because it comes back to the earth in the rainfall, our oceans, lakes, and rivers are now full of mercury and other contaminants. Mercury levels are so high that nearly all fish are contaminated with it, and I believe they are now unfit to be eaten. This is a tragedy, and, with great sadness, I made a decision a couple of years ago to no longer eat fish. Since then I have been taking organic flax oil, which provides the elements of Omega3 and Omega6 that our bodies need, and which are available in fish. I mix a little more than a teaspoon of the flax oil in some yogurt and usually put it on my cereal. It tastes great. I also use organic coconut oil. I eat it, cook with it, and put it on my skin. I grieve for the whales too, for they are contaminated with polychlorinated biphenyls (PCBs) and all manner of pollutants that have been dumped into our waters. Coral reefs are dying. Forests, the required habitat for thousands of species of animals and birds, are being decimated, and the numbers of species that have become extinct grows larger every year. All the hydroelectric projects, which have created dams, have displaced animals, birds, and other forms of life, and dramatically affected nearby trees. Animal behavior changes when forests are decimated by flooding conditions, and strange patterns have emerged. Our food sources are becoming unsafe through genetic modification. Aquifers around the planet are being depleted at an alarming rate, and water is an essential element for sustaining all life. If we do not have adequate water, life on our earth cannot continue as we know it.

Even here on this beautiful island I have watched the changes that have occurred in the fourteen years since I moved here. Except for some regulations and permit requirements, people and corporations who own property can do what they want with their property. Many wealthy people have bought up choice parcels of land on this island, cleared out beautiful trees and shrubs, built lavish homes, and "parked out" their property to make it look like the estates in the suburban areas on the mainland. In the last few months I have witnessed the total upheaval of the lovely eight-acre meadow adjacent to my apartment. Earth-moving equipment was brought in and a road was created, as well as several unsightly berms of earth. Fortunately, the owners did not remove any trees from this parcel of land. But on the adjoining land a new sub-division of homes is going in and many trees were literally shoved over and removed. I watched with horror as those trees went down. For several months we residents have had the jarring noise of drilling through rock to create trenches for the utilities and provisions for a new road. I feel the earth's pain in this process, and I mourn for the natural beauty that has been obliterated.

As I write this in 2005, climate change is evident all over the planet. I have read a great deal about global warming, and experts on the state of the earth's environment use the word "precarious." The environmental changes are extremely serious, and many scientists tell us that our planet is in peril. Scientists have drilled deep into the ice layers in the Arctic and Alaska and have taken core samples that are like time capsules. These core samples show how the ice has changed over thousands of years. Glaciers are melting, and that will cause sea levels to rise. Coastal areas will change, and an enormous amount of land will be under water. Predictions are that global warming will increase and continue to greatly affect weather patterns on the earth.

I have heard it said that history has shown major changes go hand in hand with crisis. I read that one physicist recently said a crisis can lead to a quantum leap in evolutionary development, that all of humanity is currently in a state of crisis, and we are trapped in fear and self-interest. What is required is a basic change in our attitude and priorities. Our cultures will survive only if we recover our spiritual (or higher) values. We must honor the interdependence between species on the earth. We have to recognize that we are not separate from nature, and then shift to sustainable ways of living, using renewable resources. At times the outlook is very bleak. Witness the clear cutting of forests, the constant use of chemicals and pesticides, and observe the incessant advertising for still more consumer goods. The marketing techniques are atrocious, and corporate greed is horrifying. We must stop corporate welfare in the form of subsidies or favorable treatment that is going on in this country, and tax those who are using non-renewable resources. Corporations must be held accountable for their actions and practices that pollute the environment.

I think that trend is coming; many European countries have already adopted what they call "tax shifting." This means shifting the primary burden of taxes from workers' incomes to those who use non-renewable resources. This will encourage industrial innovation. It appears that the United States will have to follow suit, so that its businesses remain competitive. It is essential that we reduce the use of coal to produce energy on the planet, which would be possible if we stop subsidizing the fossil fuel industry. We also have to eliminate child labor and the sweat shops around the world, which create enormous profit for just a few. Population control demands urgent action, and we must end war on this planet. We clearly cannot continue on the path we are on.

A serious reality is that there is a shift occurring in this country from public ownership and administration of our natural resources and services to private for-profit corporations motivated by profit, rather than service. Our democracy is rapidly eroding. Fear has been intentionally induced by our government officials, as well as other governments all over the world. People are more easily controlled when they are fearful, and that is the purpose. But in recent months I have seen phenomenal efforts by many organizations to assist in uniting us to take back our power and oppose policies that are not truthful and will not serve the greater good.

There have been some extraordinary developments in very recent years that provide hope. High frequency energies have been used to clean contaminated sites. Solar and wind energy technologies have been highly developed and much more widely used for producing energy. These developments that can produce clean energy on a massive scale and, at the same time, create an abundance of jobs and stimulate the economy are exciting to me. Just think of the impact this would have on reducing global poverty.

The technology is already available for the production of hybrid cars and buses that run on energy created by hydrogen fuel cells instead of gasoline. Fuel cells emit water vapor instead of poisonous exhaust fumes that create damage to our environment. These cars and buses have extremely high fuel efficiencies, and this would also reduce our reliance on imported gas and oil. Several auto makers already produce these new cars. Though many big corporations are fighting these developments because they believe it would result in a loss of profit, the technology is there and the public is beginning to support it. I recently read about a completely new and innovative design for cars called "Hypercars," which are propelled by a "hybrid-electric drive." As more of the new hybrid cars are produced, the prices will go down and more people will be able to afford them. This is very positive.

There is a renaissance occurring in organic farming all over the world. Organic farming is sustainable, and farmers in many countries have shown it not only increases production, it offers a wide range of ecological benefits. As crop yields have increased, it has also greatly empowered farmers. More and more people are choosing healthy food over the products that are fertilized with chemicals and genetically engineered. Farmers' markets are wonderful gathering places for buying healthy food directly from the farmer who produced it. One of my special delights from spring through early fall is to go to the weekly farmers' market on our island. I know the farmers and the high quality of their products, and I see many of my friends there. It is a joy for all of us.

I have a dream that my grandchildren will also have the joy of becoming grandparents later in their lives. If we continue to pollute our environment and allow the greed of corporations and governments that control and contaminate our air, fresh water, and other natural resources, this may not be possible. We are in an enormously critical time on the earth, and we must shift the priorities in our country. We need to treat the earth and all of nature as sacred. If we recognized the sacredness of life, we would not allow the toxic and devastating things that are taking place around the world.

In addition to the many extraordinary projects around the planet, lots of people are becoming aware and making individual choices to solve problems in a manner that honors everyone and the earth. Many books have been published, and there are two magazines (I'm sure there are many others) that I think are enormously inspiring. *Ode* and *Yes!* are filled with stories about people and communities that have created solutions that benefit everybody—and the earth. Each issue has fantastic and heart-warming stories about people sharing their talents and energy for the good of all.

A particularly inspiring book I read recently is Alan Weisman's *Gaviotas—a Village to Reinvent the World*. The reviewer writes: "Sixteen hours from the nearest major city, they invented windmills light enough to convert mild tropical breezes into energy, solar collectors that work in the rain, soil-free systems to raise edible and medicinal crops, solar 'kettles' to sterilize drinking water and ultra-efficient pumps to tap deep aquifers—pumps so easy to operate, they're hooked up to children's seesaws." The United

Nations named this village in Columbia a model for the developing world. Besides all these accomplishments I was inspired by the peaceful and honoring manner of their community toward all of its members. Their cooperative way of living together was as remarkable as their ingenious inventions. The village of Gaviotas is the kind of community I would like to live in.

In another excellent book, *Better Together: Restoring The American Community*, Robert Putnam and co-author Lewis Feldstein describe in depth twenty different community projects in our country. Public Television (PBS) has provided many outstanding programs about the environment: what is happening on the earth and what projects have been created to provide remedies to harmful policies in order that we may live in harmony with nature.

Still another inspiring book is *The Light of Conscience*. Author Bill Shore talks about moral entrepreneurs who "bring morality to places where it hasn't been before . . . They inspire new moralities altogether . . . they expand conscience . . . and they aim to remake the for-profit sector." Mr. Shore founded the national nonprofit organization called "Share Our Strength," which has raised more than $150 million to support anti-hunger and anti-poverty organizations worldwide.

There are numerous environmental groups, as well as groups that are working for human rights. I have been a member of several of these organizations for many years. Some organizations are focused on one single project in one location, while others are international in scope. I am awed by the wide spectrum of humanitarian organizations and projects that are working diligently to protect natural resources and to provide assistance to human beings in a myriad of ways. World hunger is still a reality all over our planet. There are some outstanding and effective programs currently operating in many countries that are designed to help the local residents grow and market food, as well as to distribute surplus food and supplies from other countries to those in need. Brazil and Africa have success stories that demonstrate that, by making a commitment to eliminate hunger, there will no longer be thousands of children and adults dying each day from starvation. As we are all a part of the problem, so can we all be part of the solution. When people in a community come together to create solutions to problems, remarkable and innovative ideas can emerge.

Part of the solution in this country, I believe, requires the reforming of our political system. I recently learned that some states and cities have now adopted a "clean elections" form of financing for candidates who are running for a public office. In order to qualify for clean financing, a candidate must demonstrate a broad basis of support by collecting a signature and a five-dollar donation from a required number of local voters. Those donations are then given to the clean elections fund. Qualified candidates receive a fixed and equal amount of public funds, and they are therefore not dependent on corporate donations. I understand that Maine, Arizona and North Carolina were the first states to implement this form of financing for candidates. I think this is a very exciting development, because it allows a greater diversity of candidates and releases them from the obligation of pursuing the special interests of a corporate donor after they are elected.

Also, I think we must restore and preserve local control of our media. Over the past few years a shift has occurred in this country, which has resulted in nearly all levels of our media being controlled by monopolies. This is a threat to our democracy. We must endeavor to preserve our democracy by allowing our citizens to have access to journalists and information that is not controlled by corporate ownership.

I have witnessed many neighborhood projects. I remember that when I owned my home in St. Paul for those seven years in the early 1980s, we would occasionally have big snowstorms during the winter that would dump huge quantities of snow. Sometimes there would be heavy winds as well, which would create big drifts of snow over all the cars parked on the street. After the storm passed, the snow plows would clear the main streets. All residents on side streets would be directed by city officials to move their cars to the open thoroughfares so that the snow plows could clear the side streets. My home was on a side street, and most of my neighbors parked their cars on the street, as I did, because we couldn't get into our garages. All of us would go out to the street with snow shovels and big brushes in hand. No one had motorized snow removal devices back in those days. Rather than each of us starting with our own car, we would all start working together to clear the first car in line. When it was free, and the owner had driven his car to the thoroughfare, we would all shout with joy. Once the driver of the first car had his vehicle safely parked on the thoroughfare, he would come back and help with the other cars. Then we would all start on the next car in line. Each would be easier to move than the first, because that next car could use the tracks made by the first car. Everybody continued working until all the cars were shoveled out. Even though it was often very cold, and we were bundled up in down jackets and mittens, there was wonderful camaraderie with lots of fun and laughing. These neighbors were not close friends, and no one made phone calls for help. It was just a spontaneous group project, with no leader, but each time we gathered together to accomplish the task at hand, we felt great afterwards.

I have been inspired by several people who have spent considerable time living with indigenous tribes in other countries. Marlo Morgan, who went to Australia and has had phenomenal experiences with the aborigines, and John Perkins, who has spent an enormous amount of time with tribal people in South America and Indonesia, have written fantastic accounts of their experiences. We have so much to learn from the indigenous peoples around the world.

Others will show us the way, too. I understand that there have been thousands of children born in the past twenty or so years around the world who have come into their physical bodies from the higher dimensions with very exceptional abilities. They are often called "Indigo children" or "crystal children." I believe they will be extremely important leaders in the coming years as they help to facilitate the paradigm shift. Look for books and movies about them.

We humans are enormously creative. This is a time of great possibilities on the earth. And as more and more people wake up to their spiritual nature, these efforts will expand. It will be a natural response to honor our oneness with reverence for all life. There will continue to be many ordinary people who will inspire others to focus on cooperation, to create a sense of community (without an enemy), and to seek relationships rather than confrontation. There are multitudes of volunteers working together to solve problems all over the world. No matter how controversial things get, we need to treat each other with kindness, respect, and compassion. This is being heart-centered. When we do what we do with love, it nourishes our souls. And when we nourish our souls, our lives have meaning. I have heard it said that spirituality transcends beliefs. I agree. There's a wonderful adage, I heard long ago, that says that there are many paths to the top of the mountain, but we're all trying to get to the same place. There must be a respect for diversity in our spiritual quests, and everyone must be free to follow their own path—their own unique journey of discovery. In this way we are free to grow, to discover our own spirit, and allow it to unfold.

When Krysta Gibson started my interview article back in 1987, she quoted me as saying: "There are only two reasons that we come into these bodies on the earth plane—to learn and to serve—and we learn by serving." I still know this to be true. And service doesn't necessarily mean that we have to get involved in some big and meaningful project for the planet. Some will do that. But just simple acts of kindness are beautiful ways to be of service. We often never know how much a smile, a compliment, or a small gesture of kindness has lifted the spirits of another person.

A dear friend of mine, who is now in her eighties, has a severe case of diabetes which requires that she be given an insulin injection every four hours. She has lived an active and innovative life, but now she lives in the convalescent center on the island and is very limited in what she can do. She is one of the most heart-centered people I know; I have never heard her complain. In fact, she frequently tells me how much she appreciates the care she receives. Her gratitude is awesome. Her gentle manner, radiant smile, and kind words are an inspiration to everyone. Both she and I know that she is assisting the Light, and thus she is serving the transformation of consciousness, even as she is lying on her bed. The key is her enormous capacity to love and to share it with others.

I have learned that when we open ourselves to provide services to others, it is very important that we be clear about our service and do not fall into a pattern of servitude. One of the articles I wrote for *The New Times* years ago was called, "Service or Servitude?" I think it was the most difficult article I was instructed by my spiritual guides to write because I had to learn some lessons for myself in the process. I began that article with a statement that was channeled by a friend of mine from a beautiful Ascended Master named El Morya. His statement was: *"Service is the most expedient manner of evolution; servitude is the slowest."* The challenge, of course, is to recognize the difference. I think I'm still searching for a deeper, clearer understanding about service, but I'd like to share what I have learned thus far.

There are several aspects to be explored, but let me begin by saying that I think our commitment to our growth and evolution, our efforts to achieve our highest state of evolvement in this lifetime, is through service. And to serve others is to assist them in achieving their highest potential, without placing limits or restrictions upon them, but rather allowing them their own freedom of choice. It is to hold out our hands with an attitude of "I love you, and I allow you to be the greatest, most magnificent that you can be, and I will walk with you to assist you into your full realization, if that is what you choose."

As I have said earlier, each of us has chosen the particular conditions into which we were born, and we chose them for the opportunities that were available for us to learn specific lessons. If someone has a "weakness," whether it is physical, mental, or emotional, there is a reason for it. And if we jump in and try to "fix it" for them, or carry them, we may be denying them their experience, their right of accomplishment, their own ability to work through this particular condition. Initially, we might not recognize what we are doing and how much time we are spending. After awhile some anger and resentment begins to develop. What we initially did out of love, or what we called compassion, was in truth pity. And it has turned into something that is not love, but an obligation that is done with resentment. This is servitude. If an act of service is not done freely and with love, then it is servitude.

Many people are really great at creating situations in which they can be put into servitude, and others are most willing to put them into that state. There are people who are quite satisfied with letting others do their assignments. If we willingly step in and do them, then we have denied them their growth. It is important that we carefully look at what we do. Do our actions assist another person on their path and assist them in their evolution? Or are we creeping into the corners, offering our "free" advice, and perhaps stifling or crippling them, getting in the way of their learning and robbing them of their choice?

Whenever we approach a task with a "poor me" attitude, feeling duty-bound, we have entered a state of servitude, for we have given away our power. Servitude is a state of bondage. Many people spend the majority of their waking hours in what we call duty. It is our duty to go to work, to love our parents, to love our spouse, to love our children, to clean the house, and so forth. Our whole society is based on duty, what we "should" do. How many things do we do each day out of duty, and how many of these could be done out of a total commitment of love for others and ourselves? Our attitude makes the difference. Duty requires that you do something, not in love and not in balance, but because you perceive that someone else desires that you do it. It is easy to get caught up in a sense of duty and feel like you cannot escape; but escape is possible and is really quite simple. Remembering that we are here by choice, it begins by sitting down and quietly looking at ourselves, our activities, our tasks, and then asking, "Why do I do these? How do I do these? And do I want to continue to do these?"

Look within and see what is there. Become familiar with yourself. Become your own friend. Look at your thoughts and your attitudes, and in this self-examination process you might discover that you can no longer continue to help someone because you are not doing it in love. You are doing it out of duty. If you have friends or family members who call you and plead with you, and take up much of your time, look and see if you have created this servitude. Have you created this so they are dependent on you and cannot survive without you? If so, you have placed yourself in servitude. It is not service to create another person's dependence upon you.

Search deep within yourself for your motivations. If you find that you are continually caught in servitude to others, ask, "Is this my choice? Why have I allowed another person to deny me my freedom? And why would I choose to deny someone else their freedom and bind them in servitude?" Jesus did not create servitude; he created a love of mankind and a desire to serve out of love. So our task is to learn how to love and to sow the seeds of love in all that we do. It is not to come from fear about creating dependency, but to make a conscious choice. When our motivation is fear, we are not acting out of love.

We are asked to look closely at our relationships, at our partners, friends, and loved ones. What binds you together? Are they relationships with full opportunity of expression for each of you, or are you bound by duty or obligation? Are each of you allowing the other one his or her choice, and are each of you allowing the other to grow?

Giving myself permission to choose still gets tricky sometimes. On one occasion, one of my dearest friends went to her family reunion in Boston. Before she left, she said she'd bring back some fresh-caught, live lobsters for dinner the night she returned to Seattle. At the time I thought it was a marvelous idea, and we made the date. She drove from the airport to my house with the live lobsters in an ice-filled styrofoam chest in her car. She put the chest in my bathtub, and we looked at these beautiful creatures. As I went to the kitchen to heat up a big pot of water to cook them in, I had some very uncomfortable feelings. Although at that time I still ate fish, I hadn't eaten a whole lobster for many years, and I realized I didn't want to cook and eat any of the lobsters in that chest. Even though I had originally anticipated that I would enjoy this experience, I found in the moment that this was not true.

I tried to rationalize to myself that if it were a piece of salmon or halibut, that fish would have been alive before it was prepared for me to cook. But that didn't help. My friend was feeling so much joy, and her gift was clearly an act of service out of love. She had gone to a lot of trouble and expense to bring those lobsters back from Boston, so I said nothing about my feelings and pretended that I was enjoying them as much as she was. I placed myself in servitude.

When we pretend to feel something because we perceive it as a kind and loving thing to do, or for our survival, or for whatever reason, then we deny ourselves our true feelings and our integrity. Pretending activates a warning signal that we are not in alignment with our true nature. Repeated pretending creates great discomfort and pain. If we choose to continue this pattern, then we are forced to go numb, out of touch with ourselves and our warning signals. When we cut ourselves off from our inner selves, the alternative is to go outside ourselves and look only to others as a way to function in the world. Psychotherapists call this condition co-dependency.

Co-dependency is sacrificing yourself, your sense of self, for another person or persons. It is the habitual limiting or stopping of one's full expression of self in relation to others. There are workshops and programs available to work on co-dependency issues. One of them is Al-Anon, a spiritual recovery program that helps people break the patterns and habits of binding themselves and losing themselves to others. It uses the Twelve Step Program that originated in Alcoholics Anonymous (AA), but alcohol need not be the issue in order for people to participate. The issue is co-dependency—servitude and sacrifice—creating yourself as a victim.

When we are motivated by feelings of victimization, our acts of service are not motivated by love. But when we serve out of great love, it is so beautiful. Years ago when I participated in Native American sacred ceremonies, I witnessed some of the most beautiful acts of service I have seen. I vividly remember an incident at an Indian gathering in Indiana. There were two large sweat lodges with a huge fire circle in the center between them. Two Indian men were tending the fire tirelessly, bringing the red hot rocks from the fire into the sweat lodge as the medicine persons requested them. I observed them from time to time working very hard over the three-day period of the gathering. On the third day, I happened to stand in the lunch line behind one of the men, and I told him that I appreciated his efforts very much. It surprised him. "It is my honor," he said softly, respectfully. His expression clearly indicated to me that he realized that I didn't understand. He needed no recognition or appreciation, and there was no pride in his voice. It was indeed his honor to serve out of his love for the people and for the ceremony.

I think it can sometimes be easier to serve freely out of love, with no thought of acknowledgment or reward, in a more public way than it is in the little daily services that come up. Things like having to get up early every day to make breakfast for the children and get them off to school, or let the dog out one more time, or care for an aged parent or sick friend.

Carefully look at how much they can do for themselves, being mindful that you do not smother them or deny them their growth. Then make your choice about the service that needs to be provided and endeavor to do what you choose with love and joy in your heart for the privilege of being available for that service.

We must keep remembering that we are here to learn and to grow and to serve, and that we have chosen the circumstances into which we have come. Therefore, our service is fulfillment in itself, and we need no other reward. If we expect gratitude from someone for our service, then we are placing them in servitude. As long as we can remember that each one of us is equally worthy and totally loved, just as we are right now, by the Creator, then we don't need to look outside ourselves for validation from others. There is a difference between asking for support and looking to others for validation. This is definitely a time to support each other in our growth, and that is service.

Ultimately, our purpose is to increase our capacity to love—both ourselves and others. I think most of us have the longing to love and to be loved. Unconditional love means loving without judgment. Most of us tend to judge ourselves most harshly. I have learned that the extent to which I can forgive and love myself unconditionally is the extent to which I can do that for others. Forgiveness and compassion are evidence of courage and strength, and they allow us to release fear.

It takes great courage to forgive what might be considered unforgivable, to be able to feel compassion toward those who have done harm. Forgiveness is a process, and it begins with a choice. It may require a long and deep process of grieving until you feel a release in your heart. But healing can then take place, and we can find peace. It is a process of letting go of the fears, and the pain of the wounding. Sometimes the best way to let go is to grieve. Eventually we will feel ourselves softening and becoming free, and then we can find peace. So we need to be gentle with ourselves. The greatest benefit from our act of forgiveness comes to ourselves—much more so than for the other person. Our act of forgiveness may, however, create an opportunity for the other person to open up to a whole new level of growth in their life. When I can forgive someone who has hurt me, it is nourishing to my spirit. We nourish our spirits by our acts of kindness and forgiveness. We also nourish our spirits when we fulfill our purpose, our soul's destiny.

I know that we come into these lives in order to complete lessons as well as to serve. When we have completed the lessons and service, we are free to go "Home" to Spirit from which we came. It is graduation. I have told my children and friends that when it is time for my passing on, I hope they will have a party—a celebration—for I will have graduated. I deeply know that there is no judgment on the "Other Side."

I have personally witnessed the incredible value and importance of prayer. When I was doing individual healing work with friends and clients, I always began with a prayer for the highest and best good, and remarkable things happened. I also began every group session that way. Many scientific studies have been published that show prayer does have an effect, and often a profound effect. Over the years many people have asked me how I pray. When I pray, I talk very simply to the Source, the Mother-Father-God, and I do this off and on throughout the day as I feel the impulse. Usually I begin each morning with an extended meditation and prayer-time of about a half hour or more. (At the end of my story I have included a description of my morning prayer and alignment of my intention for the day.) For some people an evening prayer-time works best, but I like to start my day feeling attuned and close to my Creator. We each have to discover what works best for us, and ultimately it is our intention that is most important.

A friend shared a brief and very powerful prayer with me some time ago. Here is what she says: *"Father, I stand before you as thy willing servant. Thank you for removing anything that stands between you and myself in its totality."* Sananda told me years ago that I was to release all that ties and binds me to this plane. That prayer makes a commitment to God that I am willing and asking to release anything and everything that keeps me limited or feeling separate. I choose to experience my oneness with the Father-Mother and with everyone and everything in creation, and I ask for help to do that, giving thanks in advance for that help. I thank God and all my spiritual guides for the blessings and gifts I have received, their love, guidance, and protection.

Every morning I align myself with the God Source and open myself to be an instrument. I then align and attune my personal will with the Divine Will, affirming my intent to keep my thoughts and actions in harmony with the Divine. I ask that the Divine Will manifest through me. I pray that Divine Love will flow through me, for myself and for all others. I reaffirm my commitment to fulfill my purpose for being here and open myself to experience whatever is required to do that. I set my intention to keep every thought and act of mine in harmony and alignment with unconditional love without judgment, with truth and honesty, with compassion, and with gratitude. Then I pray for the well-being of our beautiful earth, for its healing and re-balancing. And I pray for the best and highest good for all life on the earth—for peace and harmony among all people. I visualize and feel that peace and harmony, and I pray for the transformation of consciousness. I commit myself to assist that transformation in whatever ways I have the capacity. I also pray for the highest good for all government leaders in every country. I have a prayer list of special and beloved ones in my life, and others for whom I have been asked to pray, always asking for their highest good as they choose to accept it.

This is not a ritual. It is a very personal sharing from my heart. Then I talk about whatever is current and that I need guidance for, and go into quietness and meditation to commune and listen. It is a precious time and a wonderful way to start my day. Many creative thoughts come to me during this time, and I feel happy and peaceful. Some of the most beautiful and powerful experiences I have had in prayer have been completely non-verbal. I have felt a flow between myself and the Divine that needed no words. In fact, words would have felt intrusive in those situations. Each of us must find our own way to communicate with our Creator. There is no right way. The important thing is that prayer comes from your heart, and it helps you to open your heart and become more loving.

In the early part of 2004 I had a small stroke and was airlifted in a medical helicopter off the island to a hospital on the mainland. Friends and neighbors immediately began to pray for me, and the following evening a group of a dozen friends gathered in a home and prayed for me and for others who were in need. I was completely healed and have no residual effects from that stroke. It was caused by a small blood clot that resulted from a spell of atrial fibrillations. Again, I am most grateful. Individual and personal prayers are powerful, but when a few, or many, are gathered at one time, the results can be profound.

One of the most beloved prayers for many people, and for me, is the well-known prayer of Saint Francis of Assisi. It touches my heart and soul and expresses so simply and beautifully what I deeply know to be true.

Prayer of Saint Francis of Assisi

> Lord, make me an instrument of your peace.
> Where there is hatred, let me sow love;
> Where there is injury, pardon;
> Where there is discord, harmony;
> Where there is doubt, faith;
> Where there is despair, hope;
> Where there is darkness, light, and
> Where there is sadness, joy.
>
> O Divine Master, grant that I may not so much
> Seek to be consoled, as to console;
> To be understood, as to understand;
> To be loved, as to love;
> For it is in giving that we receive;
> It is in pardoning that we are pardoned;
> And it is in dying that we are born to eternal life.

What I have learned on my journey over all these years is that you ask for spiritual guidance and know that you are being guided, even if you do not hear words. Ask what you need to do to carry out your purpose, and allow your role to evolve. It is especially helpful to give thanks in advance for the perfect resolution to any given situation for which you are asking guidance. "Think from the end," Wayne Dyer says. Hold in your mind the vision of the outcome you desire, and imagine that it has already taken place. Don't focus on what you don't have, or what worries you. Rather, put your attention on what you want and be grateful for what you have right now. Trust that whatever will serve your highest good will unfold, and respond to the opportunities that present themselves. That is essentially what I have done throughout my life.

Meditation is essential, I think. There is no "best" or "right" way to meditate, and there are numerous books, courses, and workshops that teach a variety of ways to meditate. There are also many beautiful tapes and CDs that you can follow as you sit quietly with your eyes closed. The purpose of meditation is to help us get quiet and in touch with our inner knowing. This helps to stop the typical busy process of our mind, our thoughts, which often prevent us from accessing our intuition. Spending time in solitude is nourishing to our spirits and allows us to feel an inner serenity. We need to keep the stillness and the activity in our lives in harmony and balance. For some people soft and inspiring music facilitates this quietness; for others a person speaking and guiding the meditation process is helpful. Still for others, chanting is what works best. And some prefer complete silence. Many people prefer to meditate while they are out in nature—either sitting or walking. If meditation is new to you, experiment with it and see what helps you to access this quietness within yourself. Be willing to try different things until you discover what helps you to feel connected to your own inner being, your soul. Our souls are eternal, and in our quietness we can allow our souls to nurture us. You will more easily be able to trust your intuition as you become accustomed to quieting the "chatter."

So take time to be quiet. In our busy daily lives, that may be a challenge. We do take time, however, to feed our bodies, so we can also choose to take time to feed our soul's longings. In your solitude you may choose to pray, to meditate, or to ponder, opening yourself to awareness that comes from within, from your inner wisdom. If you ask for it, you will receive much guidance from your spirit guides. But it helps to be quiet in order to hear it, to see it, to feel it, to "know" it. It often doesn't come in words, but rather as an intuitive knowing, so don't be discouraged if you don't hear your guidance in words. Some see, some hear, some feel, and some just sense it intuitively. We each have our own way of receiving and perceiving.

Trust your intuition—your own inner voice. Feel it within yourself. Take risks, if they are in harmony with your values and your integrity. Evaluate the risk, and if it feels right and your heart is leading you, then go for it. Proceed with enthusiasm, even if you don't know at that moment how to carry out your next step. And, most important, get involved in something that inspires you, something that you feel passionate about and that helps you to feel vibrant and alive. This will bring joy and fulfillment to your life. Spend time doing what you love to do. When we focus our energy on what we love, a transformation happens. Allow your creativity to flow. Sometimes we start by being a volunteer. Focus on your commitment to be of service, to carry out your purpose. And give thanks in advance for the perfect way to provide for your needs in the process. Then allow the magic to happen. And, by the way, being of service does not mean we have to be serious. Laughter nourishes our spirits if we share it in a loving way. So have fun!

Each person's journey will be unique. My spiritual guides have recently told me that my spiritual journey has unfolded in a manner that has been a "formless form" and a "pathless path." This has not been the case for many of my friends for whom a particular course of study, group, religion, church, or practice is their unique path. There is no "right way" to proceed on our spiritual path, and I think that is great.

Many years ago Sananda gave me this message, which has been enormously helpful to me:

Walk carefully, dear one, and listen closely and carefully to the voice, the knowing that rises from within you as you take your steps forward. Let the thoughts that have expectations go—release them—and be present in the moment and follow the impulses that come to you which are in harmony with the Divine and which bring you peace.

Let this be your guidepost at all times: Do you feel at peace with the choice or choices you are making? Do you feel at peace with the thoughts that flow through your mind? Are they in harmony with your heart and your sense of purpose and direction? Do you know that your choices are in harmony with the Divine Plan? How can you find that knowing? Trust *your sense of being at peace with them, for your 'knowing' will send up the flag of warning if your commitment is to remain true to your purpose and true to your Creator-God. <u>Trust this knowing</u>, and all else will be added unto you. Go now and proceed with your tasks, always seeking that moment of silence to 'check within' and to <u>know</u> the rightness, the purity of your choices.*

I think that this is essentially what Gandhi, Rosa Parks, Martin Luther King Jr., Nelson Mandela, and many others have done. Their acts of conscience, integrity, and courage have spearheaded transformation. They truly were allowing their hearts and their intuition to lead them.

Many people I know often feel very tired and stressed, and many experience depression as well. These can be natural responses to the changes in energy frequencies, as well as to the hectic pace of life that is commonplace for so many people. Changes in energy frequencies must be integrated within our bodies, minds, emotions, and the earth. In the past I have sometimes felt very tired during the high frequency energy transmissions, but it has been rare and unusual for me to feel depressed. There was a period of time recently, however, when I had frequent days of feeling depressed, and I heard this from many of my friends also. My pace of life is not hectic anymore, so that is not the cause for me.

I asked myself what was causing this depression since I am blessed to have a sweet life. I have a lovely and comfortable home, many loving and caring friends, abundant nourishing food, and many interesting activities. I am also blessed to have good health. Although I do not have the physical stamina I had when I was younger, I have no serious physical impairments, and I have no fear of death. I look at the people I know who are struggling with major physical problems, such as cancer or diabetes, or those in wheel chairs; I look at those who have recently lost a loved one or are going through some traumatic experience. Many of them have conditions that could definitely cause feelings of depression. And yet, at that time I felt depressed often, even though I have no history with depression. At times I felt the need to be reclusive and did not want to attend group activities. This was most unusual for me. I did not go to the birthday celebration for one of my most precious friends. I just could not handle being with a group of people that particular day. When my phone rang, I sometimes did not answer it because I didn't feel up to talking with anybody. There were times when I was unable to reach out to others regularly, which was puzzling and most uncomfortable for me. The feelings of depression gradually diminished, but they do come up, briefly, from time to time, often very unexpectedly.

I think most of us are yearning for peace and harmony in our relationships, in our culture, and in our world. It can be very challenging sometimes to stay positive when we observe the violence, greed, dishonesty, inhuman treatment, and the degradation to our environment that is occurring. I know that the angelic realm, from which I have come, and the world that will emerge after the transformation in consciousness has been accomplished, are peaceful and honoring of all life forms. I continue to hold that vision and offer prayers for the unfolding of this vision, and yet the depression comes at times. I have no answers for the solution at this moment other than to encourage all of us to support each other in this process, to recognize that we are not alone, and to be grateful for what we have.

A very special friend of mine is struggling with an issue which I sense many others have had to deal with. She and her boyfriend, both of whom are about fifty, are immensely compatible on many levels, and a beautiful love has developed between them. However, prior to their meeting, each of them had embraced a very different approach to their personal relationship to God/Creator Source. One has been a conservative Christian for a long time. The other practices a more liberal non-literal version of Christianity, incorporating elements of Buddhism, Native American, and other spiritual practices. Both are deeply committed to their paths and have put God in the center of their relationship. Yet, their differences threatened the very core of their relationship.

Recently I received this guidance in relation to my friends:

My beloved one,

I am Sananda—that one who is known to you as Jesus on your plane. The struggle which your dear friends are now going through is indeed a meaningful experience which can assist the transformation of consciousness on your planet. For the crux of the issue is whether they, and others, can continue to allow their hearts to remain open and the love to flow freely between them even as there is a difference in their perceptions of the ultimate truth.

The ultimate lesson, or challenge, is to accept each other with an open heart, even though the differences exist in their individual approaches to the ultimate truth. As I have spoken before, loving one another with an open heart, without restrictions, is the paramount challenge on your plane. The transformation will be accomplished on your planet when a sufficient mass of human beings are able to embrace and practice this level of unconditional love.

Be at peace, beloved sister. All is well.

My dream, my vision, is one of peace and harmony on the Earth, with a feeling of reverence and compassion for all forms of life, and for the earth herself. Probably most people will demonstrate that only in their personal interactions, but I believe the most effective way to accomplish this on a larger scale is to connect and network with others—to create groups and communities. My heart has been so touched by the "Parents Circle," a grief support group for bereaved Israeli and Palestinian families who have lost children in the Middle East conflict. It was started by two men, one Palestinian and one Israeli, who, in their grief over the death of their children and other family members, have come together, without judgment, to try to heal their incredible wounding. They are truly demonstrating the power of love and compassion, and also the urgency for ending this conflict. I learned from a dear friend who recently went to the Middle East that there is a group of younger Israeli and Palestinian women who also come together regularly to pray for peace. The way to peace is to choose love and forgiveness over revenge. The transformation of consciousness on this planet must include an awareness and a resolve to end all wars and to reform the disparity between the haves and the have-nots all over the earth, including the United States. I believe that as long as there is abject poverty, with people who are hungry and homeless, we will not have peace.

The higher frequencies already grounded on the earth will create and support this transformation. My understanding from my spiritual guidance is that these higher frequencies will continue to expand. In recent months I have had the strong knowing that the pendulum has reached its maximum point and has reversed the swing toward creating a paradigm shift on the planet. This is fantastic! Now, in 2005, my sense is that there is a resonance among people that is developing to a much greater degree. Significant evidence of this is the outpouring of help from all over the world to the many thousands of people who lost everything when the giant tsunami swept over Indonesia in late December 2004. People's hearts opened, money was provided, and I think that many people began to pay attention to what is really important in life. And just days ago, as I write this, Hurricane Katrina swept over the Gulf States, leaving untold thousands of people homeless and many dead. Except for the horrendous disaster of September 11, 2001 in New York City, we in the United States have never experienced a natural disaster of this magnitude in recent times. Once again people and countries around the world have opened their hearts and offered help in many forms. I believe that the compassion and caring efforts that are taking place have created some hope for those who have been so deeply affected, and certainly those who are contributing their money and assistance are expanding their capacity to love. More earth changes are predicted, and people will come together in a united effort to solve problems.

On January 10, 2005, Sananda came through with this message for me, which validated my sense of knowing about the shift I have been feeling:

Beloved sister,
  I am Sananda to greet you, and I embrace you with my love and

gratitude for the work you have assisted in accomplishing.

The shift in consciousness has indeed been initiated. Great joy is being expressed in all the realms. It will be a process which will entail considerable time to fully accomplish, but there is rejoicing for the progress that has already taken place.

Take heart, beloved ones of the Light, for your efforts have not been in vain and the ramifications will be experienced throughout the Cosmos. The Heavenly Host joins with me in joy and thanksgiving. The Divine Plan of our Mother-Father is unfolding and the tide has turned.

Continue to nourish yourselves and each other, for the challenges will be great at times as the process unfolds. Support each other when resistance occurs from those who do not grasp the perfection that is beginning to unfold and fear that personal loss will occur.

All who align themselves with the Light will be provided for and will be tenderly cared for. Trust the process, beloved ones, and know that you are not alone.

No one will be punished, for our Creator honors all souls. However, those who attempt to interfere with the unfolding of the Divine Plan will have some difficult lessons. Always there will be opportunities, however, for every soul to awaken and align with the Light.

We urge each of you to get adequate rest for your physical bodies. Be gentle with yourselves and each other, and feel the love and joy we bestow upon you all. Be at peace and know that we are with you.   Adonai

Even as we are dealing with the challenges of life at this time, there is also a sense of excitement. Everything is being accelerated. Those of us who have a glimpse and a knowing about the process of change that is taking place have a great advantage. Even though we experience these challenges, we know the end result will be a glorious rebirth on our planet. Many people who do not understand the process taking place on the earth are feeling terrified about their ability to survive and the eventual outcome. I feel great compassion for them. Perhaps my story will somehow offer hope and encouragement.

Recently I saw "*Star Dreams*," a new video about crop circles. I have seen books and other videos before and have always been in awe of crop circles. This video not only shows innumerable and gloriously beautiful circles, but it has clips of observations and insights about them from people who have witnessed and studied them. I have watched the video many times, and each time I have been enormously inspired and profoundly touched. Often I will go into a deep meditation following the viewing. This also happens with friends who have come to view the video with me. We just seem to go into an altered state from viewing the circles. Some of the comments made during the video about the crop circles are:

- They are multi-dimensional symbols—concrete symbols that speak to our hearts.
- They are highly evolved symbols, which describe that which is beyond the physical.
- They are sacred geometric visual symbols of vibratory frequencies now being introduced to the planet to raise our vibrations.
- They affect the subconscious mind and bypass our rational minds.
- They affect people at a deep level. To see them is a spiritual experience, and often transforms people.
- They are a message to us from beings who care profoundly for us.
- The crop circle sightings go back to the 8th century. During this current time period they started in England in the late 1970s. There have been 10,000 reported world-wide, and there are about 300 new ones each year in England. Crop circles have also appeared in Canada, the United States, Australia, and many other areas around the world.

These crop circles and complex spiritual geometries are evocative and mysterious. Theories concerning their origins, and the motivations of those who make them vary widely. But regardless of their origin, the effect that these patterns have on our consciousness is powerful.

I learned more than twenty years ago that our planet is nearing the close of a 26,000 year cycle. That is a staggering thought for most of us. We are in the middle of a dimensional shift from third dimension to fifth dimension. The crop circles are helping us to make this shift. Everything is energy, and everything is based on energy; this is a critical time in human history as the energy frequencies are being raised. The Hopi Indian prophesies, among others, talk about our emergence into fifth dimension. To bring this dimensional shift about, we each have a purpose, and we as humans have a combined purpose.

My dream is that all humans will remember again how happy we can be without all the wealth and gadgets; that we can recognize what is truly valuable and what nurtures us; that we can embrace our diversity, no matter what color our skin or country of origin, our gender or sexual preference, our religious affiliation, or our level of wealth; that all the world's societies can find a balance between the masculine and the feminine so that the masculine no longer dominates; that we can feel and express compassion toward those with whom we disagree; that everyone can experience the joy of feeling their oneness with all that is.

As we proceed, fear and greed will begin to disappear. We will sense a harmony, and barriers will gently be allowed to dissolve. There will be less envy, less striving to be "better than" others. Cooperation, rather than competition, will be the key. Our intentions have a direct effect on matter, on what we create, and it begins with making a commitment. When we make a commitment, the necessary steps or opportunities just seem to present themselves and unfold for us. We grow through making choices, and what we give to others we give to ourselves. It comes back to us. And, ultimately, this is all about love. Love of self and love of all others.

I am reminded of a beautiful channeled message I received a few years ago from the Heavenly Host of Angels. Here is a portion of that message:

As you know, love is the answer. As you deepen in your experience of the love of our Father-Mother, you will realize that the most powerful force is one of just "being" the love that flows through you. As a result of being the love that flows through you, many acts of kindness to all will naturally occur. But it begins with this state of beingness, and not from a firm determination to go out and "do" these acts of kindness.

Continue to allow yourself to be in the Flow, to be all that you came to be. Great love we have for all of you, and we shower our blessings upon you.

I also vividly remember a particularly beautiful sacred pipe ceremony, that I held in the Seattle area many years ago, during which "Grandfather," the Great Spirit, spoke through me with this powerful statement:

Allow my love to love through you.

As I began my story, I shared the quotation from Teilhard de Chardin, *"We are not human beings having a spiritual experience. We are spiritual beings having a human experience."* I believe our souls yearn for nourishment. There is a longing in us for joy and love—a longing to experience our oneness once again with All That Is. As we open our hearts, we can feel that presence, and then share it with others.

We are in the process of preparing the cocoon for the emergence of the butterfly. It will be like a beautiful blossom opening in the future. This transformation on our planet might take awhile, or it might be accomplished in the very near future. It will depend upon us.

Epilogue

On March 22, 2005, two days after my 77th birthday, I took a nap in mid afternoon, which I usually do. I went into a very deep sleep, which is not usual for me. When I began to awaken about two hours later at around 5:00, I had an enormously difficult time waking up. I would open my eyes, and then need to close them immediately. This continued for a few minutes, until I finally was able to keep my eyes open. I felt a little disoriented, but very present. Shortly after I awakened fully, my spiritual guides made their presence known and gently asked me to get out my notebook so that they could give me a message. I share it with you now.

Dear Beloved sister,

Welcome to our realm, dear one. While you have been asleep just now we have taken you on a tour, so to speak! Being immersed in our dimension for this period of time is the reason for your difficulty in waking up from your sleep. It is not for us to tell you when you will leave your plane and come "home" once again, but you have just had a preview in preparation for your homecoming.

We, your brothers/sisters of the Angelic Realm, are enormously pleased with your story that you have been writing. It will touch many souls and "encourage and inspire them to continue on their spiritual journey," as you have written. Your life in your current dimension has been an exemplary experience for you—and for us—for in these past several years we have been able to focus energies for Mother Earth to a level that has not been attained previously. Your role in this process has been fulfilled more fully than could have been contemplated prior to your current embodiment. For this there is great rejoicing in our realm!

Beloved sister, you have blazed a trail with your service to the Light. You have created a blueprint for others to follow which will serve the process of transformation of consciousness on your beautiful planet. The frequency of energies will continue to rise until all have attained a level that will allow harmony between all the life forms on Earth.

Feel our love, precious sister, and know that we walk every step with you. We are the Heavenly Host of Angels who embrace you as one of us. Adonai

That evening, and for the next day, I felt really spacey. I was unable to connect and relate to people—even my close and precious friends. I have no conscious memory of what I experienced in this other dimension, but after waking up I felt sad, a sense of grieving. It was hard to be on this physical plane after my experience in the other dimension, because I know it was glorious and beautiful to be on the Other Side. I definitely know that none of us have anything to fear about dying in this life! Persons who have had near death experiences have told us they didn't want to come back because it was so beautiful on the Other Side. That was my feeling after this experience.

About two days later, I felt happy and enthusiastic again. The grieving had passed. For several weeks following that experience, I had other similar afternoon resting periods after which I felt that grieving sensation for a day or two. I still have not had any conscious memory of what I experience in the other dimensions, but I know that I am being prepared to assume my work on the Other Side when it is time for my passing. My intention is to continue my endeavor to carry out my purpose with peace and joy as long as I am still here in this body on the earth plane. I am content to stay as long as my purpose is served, and I KNOW it will be a total and complete joy to go home. What an incredible adventure this life is for all of us!

☆☆☆☆☆☆

Life is indeed full of surprises! On December 9, 2005, less than two months after I had this book copyrighted and several copies printed, I experienced another episode of atrial fibrillations of my heart. After following the procedures the doctors taught me long ago to stabilize my heart beat, but without success, I checked in at our local medical clinic. Within minutes I was airlifted by medical helicopter to a hospital on the mainland. I was in the hospital for three days, got stabilized, had many tests, and then was released. A friend brought me back by car and ferry to the island and to the Islands Convalescent Center (ICC).

This was not my first experience at ICC. A few years ago I fell at a wedding rehearsal, which resulted in three pelvic fractures, and was airlifted to the mainland. After leaving the hospital on the mainland, I was brought to ICC on the island. These injuries required about six weeks of therapy and healing, and in the process I became acquainted with this beautiful facility, their outstanding staff and services.

This time, after the heart episode, I expected to rest and be cared for at ICC for a few days and then go back home. But it was clear after about a month that my heart had been seriously stressed this time, and my energy and stamina level had not bounced back. Not long after that I had the strong intuitive knowing that I would no longer have the physical ability to take care of myself and my apartment as I had before. The ICC is also a nursing home, and I felt clearly guided to make application for permanent residency. A wonderful bright corner room, with large windows on the east and south, became available and I moved into it.

It was an immense task to sort out all my stuff in my apartment of twelve years. I did what I could, and several friends helped me enormously. My son, Grant, flew to the island from Minneapolis to spend a week helping me and my friends prepare for a moving sale. I appreciated them all very much, and the transition went smoothly.

I was able to bring my favorite rocking recliner chair to my new room, along with a small bookcase that is filled with my favorite books. An ample

Jean's room at ICC

windowsill now holds my precious crystals, amethyst, and other special objects. I also brought all my favorite pictures and wall hangings; artist friends hung them for me. I look out at a vast expanse of sky, trees, beautiful landscaping with flowers, lots of birds, and a nearby wooden bench that faces south. Not only that, but on clear days I have a small glimpse of the Olympic mountains. My room feels homey; it is quite wonderful. ICC is a one-story building and has five wings that fan out from the large central nursing station. There is a lovely walking path around the building, and I go walking often.

ICC is a relatively small facility which can accommodate a little more than sixty people; the medical clinic is located next door. ICC has an expansive living room, two dining rooms, beauty shop, physical therapy rooms, and a small chapel. I can choose to have my meals brought to my room, or I can go to the dining room. There is a resident dog, a couple of cats, and a gorgeous bird enclosure for several colorful parakeets. Birthdays and holidays are always celebrated, and many activities are available. In good weather they have van rides around the island twice a week. I especially enjoy the weekly yoga class and the group singing.

I have now lived here for a year, and I truly love being here. Every staff person is warm, caring, and so helpful. They are a friendly and dedicated team, and I am beautifully taken care of. They feel like family. I can come and go as I choose, and friends stop by to see me, take me to the beach, to concerts, plays, movies, and out to lunch or dinner. I also enjoy the other residents. Companionship and activities are available for everyone; there is a great feeling of community here.

There are two beds in my room, and occasionally I have had a roommate who is temporarily convalescing from an injury or surgery. It feels different to be sharing my room at these times, and sometimes it is an adjustment for me. But each woman has been delightful and we shared some fascinating discussions. Earplugs help a lot when I am sleeping.

I have noticed in the last year or so that my memory is not as good as it was previously. My ability to remember has never been as accurate as some of my family members and friends, but I can tell that there is a difference now. However, I feel confident that the stories and information contained in this book are quite accurate, because each year for more than fifty years I have written an annual holiday letter for family members and friends. As a good secretary, I have kept copies of all of these letters, and I referred to them as I was writing this book. In addition, I have written in many journals, especially the messages I received from my spiritual guides and angels over the years.

It is quite likely that my memory loss is connected with my aging

Jean on San Juan Island in 2006

process. Recently, however, I have heard quite a few young adults say that their memories are not very accurate now and they have to write everything down. My spiritual guides have not addressed this issue, but I sense that one of the factors is related to the process we are all experiencing as our bodies are integrating the new higher frequencies of energy.

Since I have come to live at ICC and have given up my former home, I have become aware that many people feel apprehensive about reaching this stage in their lives, or their parents' lives. I think they fear that aging will deprive them of their pleasures as they give up their independence. When some of my friends first learn that I am now living full time at ICC, they get this sad look on their faces and say, "Oh Jean, I am so sorry." I tell them, "Hey, this isn't so bad. They do all the cooking (including breakfast in bed every morning), wash the dirty dishes, clean my room, and do my laundry."

The real issue for many, I believe, is their fear of losing control of their lives, and their fear of dying. When we reach this stage in our lives, we have to surrender to the unknown and release the control to which we are accustomed. It's a challenge to surrender to the changes that are required and to make peace with things as they are.

Ram Dass, in his book *Still Here*, writes so beautifully about this process and the challenges he faced when he had a serious stroke in his mid-sixties. He was immediately wheelchair-bound and required caregivers of all kinds. In his book he wrote: "Facing dread of the future is an excellent vehicle for entering into the spiritual dimension."

None of us really know what changes will come in our lives and how we will be affected, but if we can stay open to allow the changes with curiosity rather than fear, we can view it as an adventure. That is how I feel—that this is my latest adventure!

The challenge is for us to love whatever happens, even if we're scared or horrified, remembering that there is a reason, a purpose that will be served by it. I am not trying to hold onto life as I used to experience it, but rather to focus on the present moment. I am one of the fortunate ones in that I am not in pain or suffering. I am very grateful for this. However, it has definitely been an adjustment for me because I have lived a very active life.

Still, I feel peaceful and happy, and I am not afraid of dying.

Since I have been here at ICC, I was present by the bedside of an island friend as he died. His immediate family and some friends were also present, and when I walked into his room I immediately and spontaneously said, "This room is full of angels!" I could feel them, and I think it brought comfort to his loved ones as within a few minutes he took his last breath. It was a tender moment. We all gathered around him after his death and silently said our goodbyes. I felt great peace there, and I believe that he was at peace.

His peacefulness reminded me of an extraordinary experience I had about thirty years ago when I went on a river rafting trip with a friend in Pennsylvania. It was the first rafting trip for both of us, and the river was considerably higher and faster than normal because of recent heavy rains. Even though we all wore wet suits and life jackets, it was quite scary in those big waves and rapids. After a couple of hours the six of us in our raft were feeling like a great team and were having lots of fun. Then up ahead we saw a high railroad trestle bridge, which spanned the river.

As we approached the two bridge supports in the river, we tried to steer the raft between them. Unfortunately, our raft slammed right into one, and the six of us were instantly thrown into the river as the raft overturned. The current was very strong, and it carried me rapidly under water for a long distance. I was running out of air in my lungs, but I never felt any fear. I remember thinking that I might die, and then I thought of my two youngest children at home who were then about ten and fourteen. I felt very peaceful— almost blissful—and I had no fear for them either.

Then all of a sudden the current popped me up to the water's surface. I could breathe. I saw the bridge we had gone under, and it was a very long way back. I still had my paddle, and I saw my friend and another person swimming to the shore on our right. They grabbed onto a tree, which was now out in the water, and yelled at me to stick out my paddle so they could catch me as I went flying by. They did catch me, and none of us died or were hurt. The two guides in kayaks and those in the other two rafts rescued our overturned raft and helped us all get safely to shore.

Everyone was so happy that no one was injured and that we did not lose our raft or paddles. We ate a picnic lunch, laughed a lot, and then it was time to get back into our rafts. The river was in the middle of a large wilderness area, and there was no way out except by the river downstream to the pick-up landing.

We were a somber group that got back into our raft. I think everyone was more subdued, as the six of us fully comprehended what we had to do. Even though we all survived, the journey wasn't over yet. I don't remember anyone singing in our raft, because we were now intently focused on safely negotiating the rapids and rocks. We had one more scary challenge before we safely reached the landing, but we made it.

As we rode back in the bus that carried us to our parked cars, there was mostly silence. I cannot speak for the others, but I remember that I was reliving that experience and all of my feelings—the initial shock, some fear, and then the blissful sense of peace as I was carried under water by the current. Later I wondered why I had not been concerned about the possibility of leaving my two young children and felt no fear for them either. But I was very clear that I had no fear of my possible death in that river. I knew I could drown, but the profound feeling of blissful peace was paramount. I have never been afraid of dying since that experience.

Very recently one of my special and dear friends on the island was brought to ICC to be cared for because she was in the advanced stages of lung cancer. Pam was then eighty and had been on a conscious spiritual path for a long time. Over the years we had shared many meditations and workshops together. In her first weeks at ICC we often sat and talked in her room, sharing many stories and sometimes laughing and giggling like school girls. She had no fear of dying, and we talked openly about the excitement we both felt in the anticipation of her going "Home" and no longer being constrained by her ailing physical body. They were wonderfully joyous times.

As she became weaker and her breathing more labored, she made the decision to discontinue all her medications, except for the morphine she needed for pain, and the use of oxygen. She definitely was ready to leave.

Her sons and many friends had been to see her, and her husband came to be with her every day. She felt complete.

Even though she was at peace about all of that, she often became very anxious and frightened in those final days when she could not breathe and felt like she might asphyxiate. She would have a moment of terror until she got her breath and could relax into it. I learned something about this process as I witnessed it with Pam. Although she had no fear of death—in fact, she welcomed it—she experienced fear during the dying process when she could not breathe. I feel this is a very natural human response. That final period did not last very long, and she slept most of the time. Her passing was gentle and peaceful.

So here I am, in December 2006, reflecting on my seventy-eight years of life and my recent transition to living in a nursing home. I feel a deep sense of gratitude for everything; I feel peaceful and contented. I have more time now to be quiet—to sit and watch the sky, to enjoy the flowers, to daydream, to talk with friends—to just BE. I rest more, and in the quietness I feel the sacredness of everything. And the great thing about it is that I am now more available than ever for my primary work—my purpose—of assisting the energy transformation on our beautiful earth.

I think when any of us have to release our independence, for whatever reason, it can be a humbling experience, and we can feel very vulnerable, even powerless. I have had to learn how to accept my need for caregiving from others, and since I had felt very independent for a long time, I had to adjust. The most unexpected result is that I feel I have more freedom now than I did before. I could never have anticipated this, and it is quite wonderful!

I knew the important thing was to keep my heart open, to accept and to make peace with my new situation, trusting that there is a purpose that will be served by this new chapter in my life. I believe our lives are shaped by what we love, so therefore my intention is to love whatever happens. That is the path that allows us to feel at peace. Love is always the key, and love is what helps us to carry out our purpose for being here.

Peace

This article was written and published in The New Times in July of 1987, but the issues I address are still relevant and valid in the year 2007. I have no better way of presenting or expressing them.

How To Deal With The Changes
by Jean Hendrickson

The changes are coming very rapidly. As the new energies are increasing and intensifying on the planet, each of us is being called upon to accommodate on many levels—in our physical bodies, our emotional responses, our mental concepts, and in our work. Many of us feel stretched to our limits. What an extraordinary time this is! It is at the same time exciting, difficult, painful, peaceful and joyful.

Lots of people are talking about energies, and many feel baffled, confused and fearful about them. There's a feeling of newness about these energies, and the truth, as I understand it, is that indeed many of the energies that we on the earth are currently experiencing are new to the planet. This earth is preparing, in stages, to enter a whole new cycle, or dimension, and this requires that vibratory levels be raised. There are new and higher frequencies being introduced to the physical plane that have not been present before.

As we approach the period of Harmonic Convergence on August 16 and 17 of this year, we are cleansing and clearing ourselves on all levels in preparation for our handling of the tremendous changes that will take place. The time is short and the pace is greatly accelerated, but there is no need to be afraid of the changes or the process of our preparation. We will be given all the resources that we need to allow ourselves to adjust and adapt, and since we're all in this together we have lots of people with whom we can share our experiences.

Resonance in our bodies

Often the most noticeable and obvious changes are in our physical bodies. The vibratory rate of the molecular structure of our bodies is changing. The very cells of our bodies are being altered in order to allow us to handle these higher frequencies. Our neurological systems are being expanded. As this happens, many of us are feeling discomfort, unbalance and insecurity. As our bodies become accustomed to the frequency changes, this discomfort will decrease.

We are literally cleansing our bodies from the molecules on out. As the molecular structure has functioned at a lower rate of vibration and our bodies have been subjected to various kinds of pollutants, we have acquired a build-up of toxins. And as the vibratory rate is raised, these toxins and decayed materials are released into our systems. The most important and helpful thing we can do is to drink large amounts of pure water, for this will allow us to flush these from our systems.

This is a time to eat light, simple foods. Many people are finding that their food preferences are dramatically changing and that smaller quantities in different eating patterns are more satisfying. What I have been guided to do is to eat lots of raw vegetables and fruits and simple foods that require a minimum of preparation; to avoid the intake of chemicals and preservatives in my food and beverages. Listen to your body and notice your physical reactions to what you eat and drink. If you want to assist your body in making these refinements, be aware of what you're feeding it. You may find that you will need or want to eliminate such things as coffee, sugar, red meats, alcohol and tobacco.

Wear comfortable, loose-fitting clothes and shoes that do not restrict your energy flow. And do not push yourself. It's very important that you allow yourself adequate periods of quietness and rest. When you are tired, don't tax your energy levels, for as we go through these changes we don't have a reserve to fall back on. You could become physically ill if you ignore your fatigue. This is a period in which you will find comfort in quietness.

During some of the intense periods of changes in my body, I have felt pressure in my head, pressure and sometimes pain in my heart, and muscle spasms. I have found it very helpful to take fairly long baths, using epsom salts in the water, to re-balance my body. Also, I take Dr. Schuessler's homeopathic biochemical tissue cell salts. When I experience aching, twitching and spasms in my muscles, I have found the magnesium phosphate tissue salt to be especially useful. Sometimes it seems essential to just stop for a little while and let my body rest and integrate the changes. Then when I have grown accustomed to the changes I can resume increased activities.

Clearing emotional issues

At the same time that we are cleansing our physical bodies, we are also clearing emotional issues as well. We need to free ourselves of the limitations that have developed through emotional responses and behavior patterns that aren't helpful anymore. They aren't bad. They've helped us survive and cope with life in the past, but now we may need to let them go. So situations are presenting themselves which focus the issues and force us to take a look at them. Some of these issues are really intense and I feel challenged, sometimes to my core.

What I have noticed, and others have reported this also, is that issues which I thought I had resolved are coming up again. That can feel disconcerting! One person asked me if I thought she was regressing when the old issues came up again. No, I do not think we are regressing. We're just clearing it at a deeper level. Remember that we are fine tuning and refining ourselves to a new level of functioning. Each time the issue comes up, the feelings are the same but we catch on quicker, we move more quickly through it, and we have more room with which to approach it. We are expanding our parameters.

We do move through some issues and they disappear for us, but some others come up again and again for us to clear at different levels. That will keep happening until at last we have no attachment to them. That process will just take as long as it takes, and try to let go of judging yourself if you think you "should" be finished with it. Actually, I've discovered that when an old issue comes up for me and I don't respond with the old emotional patterning, it gives me a framework or yardstick within which to measure my growth. That feels great.

There is a feeling of urgency about this emotional clearing, and we're moving so fast that it feels like there is no "lag" time between issues. One person said to me, "I don't have the time to assimilate one lesson before I'm dealing with the next one." As this process speeds up, we tend to feel out of control and it's **easy** to fall into a fear response. That feels to me like a perfectly normal, **human** response, but we're also being challenged to face up to and release **our** fears as well. I think it's quite likely that whatever we're afraid of will be presented to us, and this is an opportunity to open ourselves and take the risk of really looking at it. There is nothing more exhilarating for me than to confront my fear of something and then find I can release it and let it go. I love that!

Fear is probably the most paralyzing emotion of all, and it interferes with our ability to love ourselves and each other, which ultimately is where we're going. When the fears come up, that's the time to reach deep down inside yourself and connect with your faith in the Creator and the whole creative process in the Universe. I deeply believe that we are all in good and loving hands, and when I feel solid in my faith I can then take a look at my fears. I also try to reach out to my friends, acknowledge my fear, and ask for their support. I receive so much loving help when I do this, and that renews my faith.

Altering mental concepts

Along with the cleansing, releasing, and changing in our physical bodies and our emotional patterns, we are also being given new concepts about the earth and our relationship with all life on the earth and with the Universe. We're finally beginning to understand that we're all equally loved and equally worthy and that unconditional love is possible. Most of us have felt separate for so long, struggling in our own corner, trying to maintain and nurture our beliefs in whatever we have concluded is the "right" way.

We're being presented with concepts about the oneness of everyone and everything in all of creation—concepts that aren't new at all but feel new within the framework of the ways we have been taught. The days are numbered in which we can cling to our ideas and beliefs in separateness, that one group or one way to the truth is the "right" one. We're being called upon to reawaken to who we really are, to find our wholeness within the wholeness of everything.

Everything is Light, and we are Light. Every one is Light. There are no "bad guys"—just beings who don't remember that they are Light. We're just all here to learn the lessons that will help us to go "home" to that awareness, to that remembering. Whatever it takes to stretch us, to help us release our rigid patterns of belief that keep us separate and limited, is what we'll manifest for our lessons.

When we truly understand that everything is in Divine Order, that no one is a victim, that we are all just learning how to be in the Divine flow and in harmony with the Universe, then we can let go of our judgments. In releasing our judgments, we can accept our differences and open our hearts. With open hearts, we will love freely, and love is the key.

The more we can love without judging. the more easily we will flow with the changes, embracing them with joy in the knowledge that we are part of a glorious transformation in this part of the Universe. Walk in peace, my friends. I love you.

Jean's Morning Allignment

Every morning, before I get out of bed, I lay quietly there and mentally go through a process of alignment for the day, which feels very wonderful. In general, this is the process:

FIRST, I give thanks for this new day and all the blessings and joys that will be mine this day.

SECOND, I mentally go through a cleansing process of my body, mind and soul.

THIRD, I say to myself, "With very conscious choice and intent, I now align myself with the God Source and allow myself to be an instrument." Then I say, "I align and attune my personal will with the Divine Will."

FOURTH, I say to myself, "It is my intent this day to keep every thought and act of mine in alignment and in harmony with unconditional love without judgment, with truth and honesty, with compassion, and with gratitude. It is my intent today to feel happy and peaceful this day." I take a deep breath and "feel it."

FIFTH, I pray the highest and best good for the Earth and all life on the earth. I pray for peace and harmony and for the transformation of consciousness. I commit myself to work in whatever ways I can to assist this process on the earth and the emergence of the new paradigm. I pray for my family and friends by name, other persons who I know are in special need, and I pray for the highest good for all the government leaders in our country and all other countries around the world. I pray for peace and "feel" the world and all its inhabitants being in peace, harmony and joy.

I then go into meditation.

Fairly soon after I get up, I do some stretching and other physical exercises to limber up and awaken my body for the day's activities. I also bounce on my trampoline, which stimulates the circulation of all of my body systems. I thank my body for serving me so well. Following that, I create a protective energy sphere around me. Here's how I do that:

FIRST, I take a deep breath, visualizing energy from the Source coming in through my crown chakra (top of my head) and energy from deep in the Earth Mother coming in through the bottom of my feet, and all meeting at my heart chakra. I usually mentally say something like, "I fill myself with Divine Light and radiate it out to create a large sphere of light all around me." I do that two more times to complete this radiant bubble of light around me, each time saying what my intention is. THEN I ask for protection in the light through the Angelic Realm, and I thank them for this service. Other layers of light can surround this sphere of light as well, and I intentionally ground myself in the Light from the Source and from the Earth Mother.

Also, when I get in my car to drive some place, I take three breaths in the same manner, creating a bubble of light around my car. I ask for protection for myself and my car and for anyone that comes in contact with my car. You can create this protection around your home, car, airplane, boat, etc. Again I give thanks for this service of protection.

– • –

As the day unfolds and I need to make choices, I hold the intention of what I desire as an outcome, and I give thanks for the result that will serve the highest good of all.

When I go to bed at night, I feel gratitude and give thanks for all the blessings of the day. This includes all of the joyful happenings, and also the challenges that may have occurred, for I know there are no accidents. The challenges have served a purpose, even if I am not consciously aware of it at that moment. Once again, before going to sleep, I cleanse my body, mind, and soul. I also thank my body again for serving me so well. I go to sleep sending loving thoughts to all those who I know are in need, and to our beautiful earth.

Recommended Books, Web Resources, Videos and Resources

BOOKS and PERIODICALS

Berry, Thomas. *The Great Work: Our Way Into the Future*. New York: Random House, 2000

Bodine, Echo. *Echoes of the Soul : The Souls Journey Beyond the Light Through Life, Death, and Life After Death*. Novato: New World Library, 1999

Dass, Ram. *Still Here: Embracing Aging, Changing, and Dying*. USA: Penguin Group, 2001

Dyer, Dr. Wayne. *The Power of Intention*. Carlsbad: Hay House, 2004

Emoto, Masaru. *The Hidden Messages in Water*. Hillsboro: Beyond Words Publishing Company, 2004

Frankl, Victor E. *Man's Search For Meaning*. New York: Pocket Books/Simon & Schuster, 1997

Hawkins, David. *Power vs. Force: The Hidden Determinants of Human Behavior*. Carlsbad: Hay House, 2002

Kubler-Ross, Elisabeth. *On Death and Dying*. New York: Scribner/Simon & Schuster, 1997

Maclean, Dorothy. *To Hear the Angels Sing : An Odyssey of Co-Creation With the Devic Kingdom*. Herndon: Lindisfarne Books, 1994

Morgan, Marlo. *Mutant Message Down Under*. New York: Perenial/Harper Collins, 1995

Muller, Wayne. *How, Then, Shall We Live?: Four Simple Questions That Reveal the Beauty and Meaning of Our Lives.* NYC: Bantam Books, 1997

Perkins, John. *Confessions of an Economic Hit Man.* San Francisco: Berrett-Koehler Publishers, 2004

Perkins, John. *Shapeshifting: Techniques for Global and Personal Transformation.* Rochester: Destiny Books, 1997

Putnam, Robert, and Lewis Feldstein, Donald Cohen. *Better Together: Restoring the American Community.* New York: Simon & Schuster, 2003

Roads, Michael J. *Talking With Nature : Sharing the Energies and Spirit of Trees, Plants, Birds, and Earth.* Tiburon: H.J. Kramer, 1987

Shore, Bill. *The Light of Conscience: How a Simple Act Can Change Your Life.* New York: Random House, 2004

Walsch, Neale Donald. *Conversations with God: An Uncommon Dialogue.* New York: Penguin Putman, 1996

Walsch, Neale Donald. *Friendship with God: An Uncommon Dialogue.* New York: Berkley, 2002

Weisman, Alan. Gaviotas: *A Village to Reinvent the World.* White River Junction: Chelsea Green Publishing Company, 1999

WEB RESOURCES

New Spirit Journal, a monthly newspaper, Krysta Gibson, publisher. Monroe, WA. www.newspiritjournal.com

WingMakers Materials. www.WingMakers.com

(continued)

VIDEOS and DVD'S

An Inconvenient Truth (about global warming) by Al Gore
www.amazon.com/exec/obidos/ASIN/B000ICL3KG/bookstorenow58-20

Star Dreams (about crop circles) by Robert Nichol,
   Genesis Communications Corporation, 2003 - 77 minutes,
   www.stardreams-cropcircles.com

The Secret - Rhonda Byrne
   http://shop.thesecret.tv/Shops/DVD_Offer.php

Spiritual Cinema Circle
   A monthly subscription to four new award-winning movies, including a feature film, documentaries and short films that are inspirational and thought-provoking. 1-800-280-8290
   http://www.SpiritualCinemaCircle.com

Indigo: the Movie. James Twyman, Neale Donald Walsch, Stephen Simon. 1 hour 45 minutes, 2005
   http://www.indigothemovie.com

The Next Industrial Revolution and the Birth of the Sustainable Economy. by Bill McDonough & Michael Braungart, Narrated by Susan Sarandon, Bullfrog Films. 2001 - 55 minutes
   (transforming the relationship between commerce and nature)
   www.thenextindustrialrevolution.org
   Earthome Productions, PO Box 212, Stevenson, Maryland 21153

Thomas Berry - The Great Work 2002 - 50 minutes
   Documentary portraying the life and work of Thomas Berry
   www.bullfroggfilms.com

HEALING RESOURCES

Reiki Spiritual Healing System
Written by Mark Gibson, friend, and Reiki Master / 2005

The word "Reiki" is a Japanese term describing a state of harmonious balance and alignment of personal energy with divine energy, personal will with divine will, personal path with universal flow. The Usui System of Natural Healing, also known as "Reiki," is a natural or spiritual system founded by Dr. Mikao Usui in Japan during the late nineteenth century. This system, while focusing on healing on all levels, ultimately guides a person towards that state of balance between limited and unlimited, personal and transpersonal, human and divine. A person seeking to learn Reiki needs to find a properly attuned and trained Reiki master and enroll in a first-degree class. At that class the Reiki master attunes the student to a limitless source of spiritual or divine healing energy, and the student then becomes a conduit of that energy for life. Reiki energy goes to the symptom being manifested and works back to the cause, using the symptom as an access point to help the person experiencing the symptom awaken to health, wholeness, balance, and given enough time and intention, ultimately, enlightenment.

For information about classes:
The Reiki Alliance: 204 N Chestnut St., Kellogg, ID 83837
phone: (208) 783-3535
email: mailto:info@reikialliance.com

(healing resources continued)

Kofutu Spiritual Healing
Written by Frank Homan, who was the channel that brought in the Kofutu system / 2005

Kofutu is a system of spiritual growth and development that has the added benefit of a healing action. The impact of living in the material world is to force our attention on physical existence, which, in turn, takes our attention off of our true nature as spiritual beings. Kofutu symbols are representations of higher consciousness energies which, when used in the proper sequences, and with the proper intent, bring us back into contact with our true nature. Reconnecting with our spiritual roots increases the flow of universal consciousness. This increase in universal consciousness enhances our ability to let go of what we are not, so that we can become more of what we truly are. This progression towards our true spiritual identity expands our possibilities for wholeness and completion.

For information about classes, go to www.kofutu.com, or write to Ken Rice, P.O. Box 1744, Minnetonka, MN 55345, USA

Costa Rica Project
    Contact: Tom Heye
    1333 Columbia Park Trail
    Suite 220
    Richland, WA 99352
    Phone: 509-735-4444
    Email: theye@walkerheye.com

Colophon

Cover, layout and book design by Bruce Conway
Cover Painting by Willow Rose
Cover photography by Jane Buck
Published by Illumina Publishing, Friday Harbor WA

Typeset in Minion Pro with
heads and subheads in Poetica Chancery II

Printed by LightningSource
on 50% recycled 20% PCW paper